Better Homes and Gard...

65 easy projects from **HOT** designers

hip knits

Meredith₀ Books
Des Moines, Iowa

Editor: Carol Field Dahlstrom
Writer: Ann E. Smith
Pattern Editor: Gayle Bunn
Technical Editor: Susan M. Banker
Designer: Angie Haupert Hoogensen
Copy Chief: Terri Fredrickson
Publishing Operations Manager: Karen Schirm
Edit and Design Production Coordinator:
Mary Lee Gavin
Book Production Managers: Pam Kvitne,
Marjorie J. Schenkelberg, Rick von Holdt,
Mark Weaver
Contributing Copy Editor: Nancy Ruhling
Contributing Proofreaders:
Judith Stern Friedman, Margaret Smith
Photographers: Andy Lyons Cameraworks,
Pete Krumhardt, Meredith Photo Studio
Technical Illustrator: Chris Neubauer Graphics, Inc.
Project Designers: Svetlana Avrakh, Gayle Bunn,
Lily Chin, Zandy Engelhart, Lidia Karabinech,
Valerie Love, Charlotte Quiggle, Ellen Sheckler,
Ann E. Smith, Kathy Zimmerman
Technical Assistant: Judy Bailey
Photostyling Assistant: Donna Chesnut
Editorial Assistant: Cheryl Eckert

Meredith® Books
Editor in Chief: Linda Raglan Cunningham
Design Director: Matt Strelecki
Managing Editor: Gregory H. Kayko
Executive Editor: Jennifer Dorland Darling

Publisher: James D. Blume
Executive Director, Marketing: Jeffrey Myers
Executive Director, New Business
Development: Todd M. Davis
Executive Director, Sales: Ken Zagor
Director, Operations: George A. Susral
Director, Production: Douglas M. Johnston
Business Director: Jim Leonard

Vice President and General Manager:
Douglas J. Guendel

Better Homes and Gardens® Magazine
Editor in Chief: Karol DeWulf Nickell

Meredith Publishing Group
President, Publishing Group: Stephen M. Lacy
Vice President-Publishing Director: Bob Mate

Meredith Corporation
Chairman and Chief Executive
Officer: William T. Kerr

In Memoriam: E.T. Meredith III (1933–2003)

hip knits

All of us at Meredith® Books are dedicated to
providing you with information and ideas to
create beautiful and useful projects. We welcome
your comments and suggestions. Write to us at:
Meredith Books, Crafts Editorial Department,
1716 Locust Street—LN120, Des Moines, IA
50309-3023.

If you would like to purchase any of our crafts,
cooking, gardening, home improvement, or
home decorating and design books, check
wherever quality books are sold. Or visit us at:
bhgbooks.com

Cover Photograph: Pete Krumhardt

cast on!

Whether you are casting on for the first time or have been a knitter for many years, you're in for a treat! Big needles, baby booties, chunky fibers, classy jackets, sequin yarn, striped socks, rich colors, retro belts, chinchilla yarn, chic sweaters—you'll find this and more in this book of easy knitting. We've included the newest fibers from the top yarn companies and the hottest colors on the shelf—and we've asked the most talented designers to create their greatest patterns. (There's even some crochet for you to try!) So whether you want to make granny-square bags, pom-pom hats, angora pullovers, baby cardigans, tank tops, cabled sweaters, bright blue mittens, an evening stole, or a boyfriend sweater, you'll find it all here! Happy knitting!

Carol Field Dahlstrom

contents

Our thanks to these world-renowned designers
for sharing their extraordinary creations with us.
We hope you enjoy using your talents to re-create
their inspiring knit and crochet designs.

meet our

ANN E. SMITH Designer, author, pattern editor, and columnist, Ann has been a contributor to the yarn industry for 18 years, sharing her skills through many industry venues. A degree in Home Economics with an emphasis in textiles and clothing construction from Oklahoma University plus graduate work at Kansas University prepared Ann for her career. You can find more of Ann's designs in *Knitting Year-Round* (Meredith) and *Crochet for Kids* (Taunton Press).

GAYLE BUNN At age 7 Gayle learned the art of knitting and crochet from her grandmother. Speedy stitches are a must for this prolific knitter who designs as many as 100 items a year for North American yarn companies and magazines. Gayle finds inspiration all around her and enjoys experimenting with different needle and hook methods. Current fashion inspires her color, yarn, and design choices and she uses vintage fashion as a reference point.

SVETLANA AVRAKH Svetlana is originally from Latvia, where knitting was a big part of her life. After receiving a masters degree in Architecture, her creativity in knitting soared. She joined Coats Patons in 1996 as a designer and writer, using her knowledge of shape and color. Find more of Svetlana's designs in *Vogue Knitting*, *Family Circle*, *Better Homes and Gardens*, *Crochet Fantasy*, *INKnitters*, and *Knitting* digest magazines as well as in *Patons Bernat* and *Lily* books.

LILY CHIN Named a "Master Knitter" by *Vogue Knitting*, this New York City native has been involved in the fashion industry since age 13. Lily designs knitting and crochet for magazines and yarn companies and develops fabric (plans the stitches) and knit downs (works out samples) for the Gap, Diane von Furstenberg, and others. Along with being a columnist, lecturer, and designer, Lily is an author. Look for her latest book, *Knit and Crochet with Beads*, by Interweave Press.

KATHY ZIMMERMAN Kathy has been designing sweaters and other knitted items for 10 years. She loves to think of herself as the cable queen—and she loves to combine cable and textured work. Her work has appeared in *Knit It!*, *Interweave*, and other knitting publications. She owns and operates a knitting shop in Pennsylvania where she lives near a ski resort with her husband and dog. She enjoys the winter and wearing her beautiful knitted wool creations.

VALERIE LOVE Born in Scotland, Val now calls New York home. She was taught as a child to knit, crochet, and sew. She studied at the Reigate School of Art, in Surrey and is a graduate of the London College of Printing, studying graphic design. During her career, Val designed knitted and crocheted decorations, working with people in England's rural areas to make multiples (some sold at Harrods in London). Val's background in graphics is reflected in the simplicity of her knit and crochet designs.

7

hot designers

outdoor

Get ready to dress for the season with fun-to-knit, great-to-wear fashions. Beat the chill of wintry days with textured scarves, colorful sweaters, and toasty mitten and hat sets. For summer outings, knit a sporty sleeveless top for you or a cotton dress in striking red, white, and blue for a little girl. Whatever the climate, this chapter offers more than 20 comfortable knits for fabulous out-and-about days.

play

9

OH-SO-HIP SCARVES

Variegated, checked, or finished with a fringe, these colorful scarves jazz up any jacket. Because they knit up so quickly, you'll want to make one of every style. Instructions begin on page 38.

stylin'

VERY COOL V-NECK

Casual and comfortable, this simple sweater is graced with garter-stitch ribs. The v-neck, three-quarter-length sleeves, and cropped hem make this a favorite to wear. Instructions begin on page 39.

relaxed

COZY

TWEEDY TWOSOME

Embellished with textured cables, this tweed duo is a must-have for cool weather. The long button-up jacket has rolled cuffs and is edged with wispy fringes. The hat is finished with a pom-pom tied to the top. Instructions begin on page 41.

ROUGH AND READY RAGLAN

Four colors of yarn add plenty of pattern to this sweater with vivid bronze and copper stripes. The raglan sleeves have more subtle stripes of dark sage. Instructions begin on page 43.

striped

cabled

WINTER SKY PULLOVER

The crewneck on this handsome wool pullover

is a perfect match for a turtleneck underneath.

The central cable adds classy flair to the front.

Wide ribbing finishes the neck and cuffs.

Instructions begin on page 45.

earthy

COLORWORK TURTLENECK

Rich fall colors, appearing as dotted rows, weave their way through this slightly cropped turtleneck. Multi-color bands lend a striped appearance to the hem, collar, and cuffs. Instructions begin on page 47.

OCEAN WAVES AND SUNSHINE HALTER TOPS

Whatever your sport, you'll keep your cool in these cotton sweaters. The V-neck, below, has a three-tone striped body. The halter, opposite, blends tube-top comfort with convenient tie straps. Instructions begin on page 48.

sporty

soft

ORANGE PEEL SWEATER

*Worked on circular
knitting needles, this brilliant
cap-sleeve sweater is styled
with a yoke and high collar.
When the autumn sun
shines, this lightweight sweater
will keep the breeze at bay.
Instructions begin on page 52.*

REVERSIBLE TWEED AND QUICK-AND-EASY SCARVES

A scarf wraps you in style and warmth all at once! Knit this pair for anyone— with or without fringe. The tweed look is created by combining solid and variegated yarns. The fringed scarf uses two solid colors to create a vertical stripe. Instructions begin on page 53.

playful

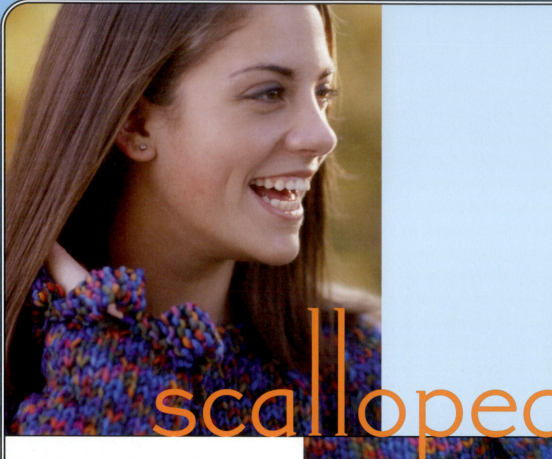

scalloped

KALEIDOSCOPE RAGLAN

Blue and purple back a sea of bright color stitches on this cute wool/nylon crop top. Scalloped hems on the body and sleeves make this sweater fun and stylish. Knit on large needles, the top is surprisingly quick and easy to make. Instructions begin on page 54.

ALL-AMERICAN DRESS AND HAT

Dress your little patriot in the colors of the flag. The cotton dress ties at the shoulders and has a slightly ruffled hem. The cap has a rolled stockinette-stitch edge. *Instructions begin on page 55.*

patriotic

TOO-CUTE COWL-NECK

Knit with soft wool yarn, this classic cowl-neck sweater features tapered sides for extra flair. With garter-stitch accents at the hems, this beauty is an easy project for any knitter. *Instructions begin on page 57.*

sassy

cuddly

COTTON CANDY JACKET AND BOOTIES

Worked in one piece, this hooded jacket is a joy to make.
Sizes range from newborn to one year. The loopiness
of the design eliminates the need for buttonholes and allows a button
to easily push through the fabric. The booties are sized to fit
newborns to six-month-olds and have twisted-yarn lace accents.
Instructions begin on page 58.

TRUE COLORS ZIP-UP

The bold variegated features of this hooded sweater stand out beautifully against a block of bright yellow. Knit with stockinette stitches on large needles, this vivid sweater works up quickly. Instructions begin on page 60.

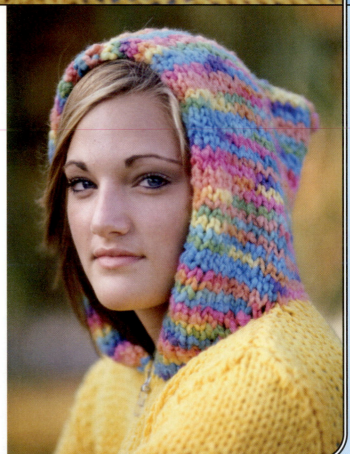

bright

CANDY-CANE COZIES

Keep little ones warm and happy with a striped hat and mitten set that resembles holiday candy. The fringe ties and dangling pom-pom make this toddler set irresistible. Instructions begin on page 62.

precious

fringed scarf

checked scarf

oh-so-hip scarves

fringed scarf

photos on pages 10–11

SKILL LEVEL: Easy

SIZE: Approximately 5 × 60", excluding fringe

MATERIALS:
Muench Yarns, Sierra, 77% wool/23% nylon, bulky-weight yarn (50 grams per ball): 6 balls of Purple/Eggplant/Multi (G153–005)
Size 13 (9 mm) knitting needles or size needed to obtain gauge
Size I/9 (5.5 mm) crochet hook

GAUGE:
In St st (knit RS rows, purl WS rows), 10 sts and 14 rows = 4"/10 cm.
TAKE TIME TO CHECK YOUR GAUGE.

INSTRUCTIONS:
Cast on 13 sts.
Row 1 (WS): K3, p7, k3.
Row 2: Knit.
Rows 3–14: Rep Rows 1–2.
Row 15 (WS): Knit.
Row 16: Knit.
Rep Rows 1–16 until piece measures approx 60" long, ending with Row 14. Bind off.

Fringe
Cut 2 strands of yarn measuring 11" long. Fold in half to form a loop. With WS of scarf facing and crochet hook, take loop through first st at lower edge. Take ends through loop and pull up to tighten. Add fringe evenly around entire scarf.

checked scarf

photo on page 11

SKILL LEVEL: Easy

SIZE: Approximately 7 × 57", excluding fringe

MATERIALS:
Lion Brand, Kool Wool, 50% merino wool/50% acrylic, chunk-weight yarn (60 yards per ball): 3 balls of Khaky (124) for color A and 2 balls of Grass (130) for color B
Size 10½ (6.5 mm) knitting needles or size needed to obtain gauge
Size K/10½ (6.5 mm) crochet hook

GAUGE:
In Color Pattern, 14 sts and 15 rows = 4"/10 cm.
TAKE TIME TO CHECK YOUR GAUGE.

ABBREVIATIONS:
Sl 1: Slip next stitch purlwise and with yarn on WS of fabric.
Sl 3: Slip next 3 stitches purlwise and with yarn on WS of fabric.

STITCHES USED:
Color Pattern (a multiple of 4 sts + 1 st; a rep of 8 rows)
Row 1 (WS): With A, k1, p across, ending k1.
Row 2: With B, k1, sl 1; * k1, sl 3; rep from * across, ending k1, sl 1, k1.
Row 3: With B, k1; * p3, sl 1; rep from * across, ending p3, k1.
Row 4: With A, k2; * sl 1, k3; rep from * across, ending sl 1, k2.
Row 5: As Row 1.
Row 6: With B, k1; * sl 3, k1; rep from * across.
Row 7: With B, k1, p1; * sl 1, p3; rep from * across, ending sl 1, p1, k1.
Row 8: With A, k4; * sl 1, k3; rep from * across, ending k1.
Rep Rows 1–8 for Color Pattern.

variegated scarf

INSTRUCTIONS:
With color A, cast on 25 sts. Work Color Pattern to approx 57" from beg, ending with Row 1 or Row 5. Bind off. Block scarf to measurements.

Fringe
Cut 3 strands of A measuring 10" each. Fold in half to form a loop. With WS of fabric facing and crochet hook, take loop through first st at right edge. Take ends through loop and pull up to tighten. Alternating colors, add 11 fringe along each edge. Trim ends.

variegated scarf

photos on page 11

SKILL LEVEL: Beginner

SIZE: Approx 6¾ × 62"

MATERIALS:
Berroco Chinchilla, 100% rayon, worsted-weight yarn (77 yards per ball): 4 balls of Lapis Lazuli (5862)

Size 11 (8 mm) knitting needles or size needed to obtain gauge

GAUGE:
With a double strand of yarn in Garter Stitch (knit every row), 12 sts and 13 rows = 4"/10 cm.
TAKE TIME TO CHECK YOUR GAUGE.

INSTRUCTIONS:
With 2 strands of yarn held together, cast on 20 sts. Knit every row for Garter Stitch until piece measures approx 62" from beg. Bind off all stitches.

very cool v-neck

photos on pages 12–13

SKILL LEVEL: Easy

SIZES: XS (S, MEDIUM, L, XL)
Note: The pattern is written for the smallest size with changes for larger sizes in parentheses. When only one number is given, it applies to all sizes. For ease in working, before you begin, circle the numbers pertaining to the size you are knitting.

FINISHED MEASUREMENTS:
Bust: 34 (36, 38, 40, 42)"
Length: 21 (21½, 22, 22½, 23)"

MATERIALS:
Brown Sheep, Cotton Fleece, 80% cotton/20% merino wool, DK-weight yarn (215 yards per skein): 4 (5, 5, 6, 6) skeins of Rue (CW375)
Size 6 (4 mm) knitting needles or size needed to obtain gauge; size 6 circular needle, 16" length
One stitch marker
Tapestry needle

GAUGE:
In Body Pattern, 20 sts and 32 rows = 4"/10 cm.
TAKE TIME TO CHECK YOUR GAUGE.

SPECIAL ABBREVIATIONS:
Ssk: Slip next 2 sts knitwise, one at a time to right-hand needle, insert tip of left-hand needle into fronts of these 2 sts and k them together.
M1: Lift running thread before next stitch onto left-hand needle and knit

in its back loop to make one stitch.

Sssk: Slip next 3 sts knitwise, one at a time to right-hand needle, insert tip of left-hand needle into fronts of these 3 sts and k them together.

STITCHES USED:
Body Pattern (any multple; a re of 4 rows)
Row 1 (WS): Purl.
Row 2: Knit.
Row 3: Knit.
Row 4: Knit.
Rep Rows 1–4 for Body Pattern.

INSTRUCTIONS:
BACK
Beg at lower edge, cast on 86 (90, 96, 100, 106) sts. Knit 9 rows for Garter Stitch Border. Beg Body Pattern and work even to approx 2" from beg, ending with Row 1.
Side Shaping
Dec Row: K1, ssk, k to last 3 sts, k2tog, k1. Work 7 rows even. Rep last 8 rows 3 times more—78 (82, 88, 92, 98) sts. Work 16 rows even, ending with Row 1. Piece should measure approx 8" from beg.

Inc Row: K1, M1, k to last st, M1, k1. Work 7 rows even. Rep last 8 rows 3 times more—86 (90, 96, 100, 106) sts. Cont in Body Pattern until piece measures approx 13½" from beg, ending with a WS row.
Armhole Shaping
Bind off 6 sts at beg of next 2 rows. **Dec Row:** K1, ssk, k to last 3 sts, k2tog, k1. Rep Dec Row every other row 6 (7, 9, 9, 11) times more. Work even on rem 60 (62, 64, 68, 70) sts to approx 21 (21½, 22, 22½, 23)" from beg, ending with a WS row.
Shoulder and Neck Shaping
Bind off 5 (5, 6, 6, 7) sts each shoulder edge twice and 5 (6, 5, 7, 6) sts each shoulder edge once. Bind off rem 30 sts for back neck.

FRONT
Work as for Back until piece measures approx 15 (15½, 16, 16½, 17)" from beg, ending with Row 4. With an equal number of sts on each side, place a marker to indicate center. P to marker, join a new ball of yarn and p to end.

V-Neck Shaping
Working sides separately and at the same time, cont armhole shaping if necessary. **Dec Row 1:** Work across to last 3 sts, k2tog, k1; for second side, k1, ssk, work to end. **Row 2:** K across to last 2 sts, p2; for second side, p2, k to end. **Dec Row 3:** In est pattern, k to last 4 sts, k3tog, k1; for second side k1, sssk, work to end. **Row 4:** Purl. Rep Rows 1–4 twice more. Cont in est pattern, dec 1 st each neck edge every other row 6 times. Work even on rem 15 (16, 17, 19, 20) sts for each shoulder to same length as Back.
Shoulder Shaping
As for Back.

SLEEVES (make two)
Beg at lower edge, cast on 50 (50, 52, 54, 54) sts. K 9 rows for Garter St Border. Beg Body Pattern with Row 1. Including new sts into pattern as they accumulate, work Inc Row as for Back every 8th row 0 (0, 4, 7, 13) times, every 12th row 0 (7, 5, 3, 0) times, and every 16th row 5 (0, 0, 0, 0) times. Work even on 60 (64, 70, 74, 80) sts to approx 12½ (13, 13½, 14, 14½)" from beg, ending with a WS row.
Sleeve Cap Shaping
At each armhole edge, bind off 6 sts. **Dec Row:** K1, ssk, k to last 3 sts, k2tog, k1. Rep Dec Row every other row 6 (7, 9, 9, 11) times more. Work 12 rows even on the 34 (36, 38, 42, 44) sts. Rep Dec Row every other row 10 (10, 10, 11, 12) times. At beg of next 2 rows, bind off 2 (3, 4, 4, 4) sts. Bind off rem 10 (10, 10, 12, 12) sts.

40

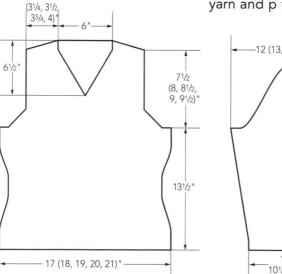

3
(3¼, 3½, 3¾, 4)"
6"
6½"
7½ (8, 8½, 9, 9½)"
13½"
17 (18, 19, 20, 21)"

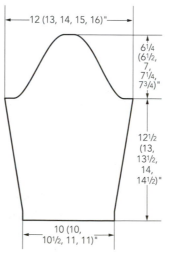

12 (13, 14, 15, 16)"
6¼ (6½, 7, 7¼, 7¾)"
12½ (13, 13½, 14, 14½)"
10 (10, 10½, 11, 11)"

FINISHING

Join shoulder seams.
Set in sleeves.
Join underarm and side seams.

Neckband

With RS facing and circular needle, pick up and k 30 sts along back neck, 32 sts along first side of V-neck and 32 sts along second side of V-neck —92 sts. Place a marker to indicate beg of rnd. P 2 rnds. Bind off knitwise.

tweedy twosome

photo on page 14

SKILL LEVEL: Easy

SIZES: XS (S, MEDIUM, L, XL)
Note: The pattern is written for the smallest size with changes for larger sizes in parentheses. When only one number is given, it applies to all sizes. For ease in working, before you begin, circle the numbers pertaining to the size you are knitting.

FINISHED MEASUREMENTS:
Bust (buttoned): 40 (44, 48, 52, 56)"
Length: 25 (25½, 26, 26½, 27)"

MATERIALS:
Muench Yarns, Tessin, 43% wool/35% acrylic/22% cotton, bulky-weight yarn (110 yards per ball): 12 (13, 15, 17, 19) balls of White/Primary (M375–801) for jacket and 2 balls for cap
Size 10 (6 mm) knitting needles or size needed to obtain gauge
Size 9 (5.5 mm) knitting needles
Cable needle (cn)
Five ¾-inch-diameter buttons
Two stitch markers
Yarn needle
Size H/8 (5 mm) crochet hook

GAUGE:
In Body Pattern with larger needles, 16 sts and 23 rows = 4"/10 cm.
TAKE TIME TO CHECK YOUR GAUGE.

SPECIAL ABBREVIATIONS:
K1b: Knit in back of the next stitch.
Pm: Place marker
Ssk: Slip next 2 sts knitwise, one at a time to right-hand needle, insert tip of left-hand needle into fronts of these 2 sts and k them together.
M1: Lift running thread before next stitch onto left-hand needle and knit in its back loop to make one stitch.

STITCHES USED:
Body Pattern (a multiple of 2 sts + 1 st; a rep of 2 rows)
Row 1 (WS): Purl.
Row 2: K1; (p1, k1b) across, ending p1, k1.
Rep Rows 1–2 for Body Pattern.

Cable Panel (over 11 sts; a rep of 12 rows)
Row 1 (WS): Purl.
Row 2: P2, k2, p1, k1b, p1, k2, p2.
Rows 3–10: Rep Rows 1-2.
Row 11: Rep Row 1.
Row 12: P2, place next 5 sts onto cn and hold at back of work, k2, (p1, k1b, p1, k2) from cn, p2.
Rep Rows 1–12 for Cable Panel.

INSTRUCTIONS:
BACK

Beg at lower edge with larger needles, cast on 81 (89, 97, 105, 113) sts. Work Body Pattern to approx 16.5" from beg, ending with a WS row.

Armhole Shaping

Bind off 6 (9, 11, 14, 16) sts at beg of next 2 rows—69 (71, 75, 77, 81) sts. Keeping 1 st each edge in St st (knit RS rows, purl WS rows), cont in est pattern to approx 24 (24½, 25, 25½, 26)" from beg, ending with a WS row.

Neck Shaping

Pattern across first 24 (25, 26, 27, 28) sts, join a new ball of yarn and bind off center

41

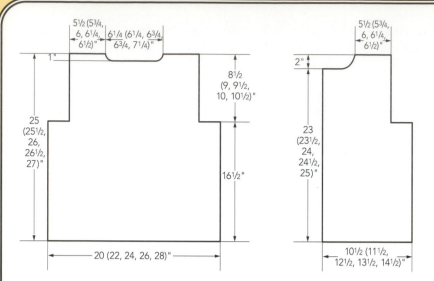
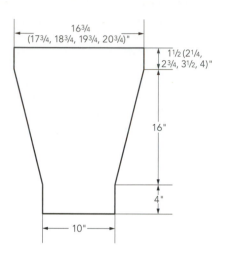

21 (21, 23, 23, 25) sts, work to end of row. Working sides separately and at the same time, dec 1 st each neck edge twice. Cont in pattern on 22 (23, 24, 25, 26) sts for each shoulder until piece measures approx 25 (25½, 26, 26½, 27)" from beg, ending with a WS row. Bind off knitwise.

LEFT FRONT
Beg at lower edge with larger needles, cast on 42 (46, 50, 54, 58) sts. **First Row (WS):** K5 for Garter St Border, Row 1 of Body Pattern across. **Second Row:** Row 2 of Body Pattern across, ending k5. Pattern is now set. Work even to approx 4" from beg, ending with a WS row.
Set Up for Cable Pattern
Work est pattern on first 13 (15, 17, 21, 23) sts, pm, Row 2 of Cable Panel across next 11 sts, pm, est pattern to end. Pattern is now set. Cont in pattern to approx 16½" from beg, ending with a WS row.
Armhole Shaping
Bind off 6 (9, 11, 14, 16) sts at beg of next row—36 (37, 39, 40, 42) sts. Keeping 1 st

each edge in St st, cont in pattern to approx 23 (23½, 24, 24½, 25)" from beg, ending with a RS row.
Neck Shaping
Bind off at neck edge, 8 (8, 9, 9, 10) sts once, 3 sts once, 2 sts once, and 1 st once. Cont even on rem 22 (23, 24, 25, 26) sts to same length as Back, ending with a WS row. Bind off knitwise.
　Place markers for 5 buttons with first 1" from neck edge and last 6 (6½, 7, 7½, 8)" above lower edge. Space remaining 3 markers 3½" apart.

RIGHT FRONT
Beg at lower edge with larger needles, cast on 42 (46, 50, 54, 58) sts. **First Row (WS):** Row 1 of Body Pattern across, ending k5 for Garter St Border. **Second Row:** K5, Row 2 of Body Pattern to end. Pattern is now set. Work even to approx 4" from beg, ending with a WS row.
Set Up for Cable Pattern
Work est pattern on first 18 (20, 22, 22, 24) sts, pm, Row 2 of Cable Panel across next 11 sts, pm, est pattern to end. Pattern is now set.

When piece measures approx 6 (6½, 7, 7½, 8)" from beg, end with a WS row.
Buttonhole Row: K2, yo, k2tog, pattern to end. Rep Buttonhole Row 4 times more, matching to markers from Left Front. Reversing armhole and neck shaping, complete as for Left Front.

POCKETS (make two)
With larger needles, cast on 21 sts. Work Body Pattern until pocket measures approx 6" from beg, ending with a WS row. Bind off.

SLEEVES (make two)
Beg at the cuff with larger needles, cast on 41 sts. Knit every row for Garter St to approx 4" from beg. Beg Body Pattern. Including new sts into pattern as they accumulate, inc 1 st each edge every 4th row 0 (2, 7, 13, 20) times, every 6th row 9 (13, 10, 6, 1) time(s), and every 8th row 4 (0, 0, 0, 0) times. Cont in pattern on 67 (71, 75, 79, 83) sts to approx 21½ (22¼, 22¾, 23½, 24)" from beg, ending with a WS row. Bind off.

FINISHING

Position pockets onto each front, placing bottom at lower edge of front and matching ribs along sides. Sew in place. Join shoulder seams.

Collar

With RS facing and smaller needles, pick up and k21 (21, 23, 23, 25) sts along back neck; turn. **Row 2 (RS of collar):** Knit across, pick up 3 sts from neck edge; turn. Rep Row 2, 9 times more—51 (51, 53, 53, 55) sts. Pick up and k 4 (4, 5, 5, 6) sts before Garter St Band on next 2 rows—59 (59, 63, 63, 67) sts. Knit 4 rows. **Inc Row:** K1, M1, k across to last st, M1, k1. Rep Inc Row every 4th row twice more and every 6th row twice— 69 (69, 73, 73, 77) sts. AT THE SAME TIME, when piece measures approx 3½" from beg, change to larger needles. Cont in Garter St until collar measures approx 6" from beg, ending with a WS row. Bind off loosely and knitwise.

Set in sleeves, sewing tops of sleeves to bound off sts at underarms for square armholes. Join underarm and side seams, reversing seam on last 3" of sleeve for the cuff.

Fringe

Cut 2 strands of yarn measuring 4" each. Holding strands tog, fold in half to form a loop. With crochet hook, take loop through first st at pocket top; take ends through loop and pull up to tighten. Add fringe to alternate sts along each pocket top. Trim ends. Using a pin, fray ends. In the same manner, add fringe around the collar; do not fray. For lower edge, cut 2 strands measuring 4½" each; add as before without fraying. Sew buttons opposite buttonholes.

CAP

With larger needles, cast on 11 sts. Work Cable Panel 9 times, then rep Rows 1–11. Bind off in pattern. With the RS facing and larger needles, pick up and k61 evenly spaced along one long edge. K 19 rows.

Shaping

Row 1 (RS): K13, ssk, k2tog, k27, ssk, k2tog, k13.
Rows 2-4: K57.
Row 5: K12, ssk, k2tog, k25, ssk, k2tog, k12.
Rows 6-8: K53.
Row 9: K11, ssk, k2tog, k23, ssk, k2tog, k11.
Rows 10-12: K49.
Row 13: K10, ssk, k2tog, k21, ssk, k2tog, k10.
Row 14: K45.
Row 15: K9, ssk, k2tog, k19, ssk, k2tog, k9.
Row 16: K41.
Row 17: K8, ssk, k2tog, k17, ssk, k2tog, k8.
Row 18: K37.
Row 19: K7, ssk, k2tog, k15, ssk, k2tog, k7.
Row 20: K33.
Row 21: K6, ssk, k2tog, k13, ssk, k2tog, k6.
Row 22: K29.
Row 23: K5, ssk, k2tog, k11, ssk, k2tog, k5.
Row 24: K25.
Row 25: K4, ssk, k2tog, k9, ssk, k2tog, k4.
Row 26: K21.
Row 27: K3, ssk, k2tog, k7, ssk, k2tog, k3.
Row 28: K17.
Row 29: K2, ssk, k2tog, k5, ssk, k2tog, k2.
Row 30: K13.
Row 31: K1, ssk, k2tog, k3, ssk, k2tog, k1.
Row 32: K9.
Row 33: Ssk, k2tog, k1, ssk, k2tog.
Row 34: K5.

Bind off 5 sts. Cut yarn, leaving a 12" tail. Thread tail into yarn needle and back through bound-off sts; pull up to tighten. Sew back seam with same tail. Cut 10 strands of yarn measuring 12" each. With crochet hook, take strands through tip of cap with an equal amount showing on each side. Tie into an overhand knot. Trim ends.

rough and ready raglan

photo on page 15

SKILL LEVEL: Easy

SIZES: Child's EIGHT (10, 12, 14)
Note: The pattern is written for the smallest size with changes for larger sizes in parentheses. When only one number is given, it applies to all sizes. For ease in working, *before you begin,* circle the numbers pertaining to the size you are knitting.

FINISHED MEASUREMENTS:
Chest: 36 (38, 40, 42)"
Length: 20 (21, 22, 23)"

MATERIALS:
Coats & Clark, Red Heart Classic Multi Color, 100% acrylic, worsted-weight yarn (3 ounces per skein): 3 (3, 4, 4) skeins of Camouflage (0971) for A
Coats & Clark, Red Heart, Classic, 100% acrylic, worsted-weight yarn (3½ ounces per skein): 3 (3, 4, 4)

43

skeins of Dark Sage (0633) for B; for all sizes, 1 skein each of Bronze (0286) for C, and Copper (0289) for D
Size 8 (5 mm) knitting needles or size needed to obtain gauge
Size 6 (4 mm) circular needle, 16"-length
Three stitch holders
Two safety pins
Yarn needle

GAUGE:
In Body Pattern with larger needles, 17 sts and 28 rows = 4"/10cm.
TAKE TIME TO CHECK YOUR GAUGE.

SPECIAL ABBREVIATIONS:
Ssk: Slip next 2 sts knitwise, one at a time to right-hand needle, insert tip of left-hand needle into fronts of these 2 sts and k them together.
M1: Lift running thread before next stitch onto left-hand needle and knit in its back loop to make one stitch.

STITCHES USED:
Body Pattern (a multiple of 2 sts + 1 st; a rep of 32 rows)
Row 1 (RS): With B, knit.
Row 2: With B, p1; (k1, p1) across.
Rows 3–4: As Rows 1-2.
Rows 5–7: With A, knit.
Row 8: With A, p1; (k1, p1) across.
Rows 9–12: With C, rep Rows 1–4.
Rows 13–16: As Rows 5-8.
Rows 17–20: With B, rep Rows 1–4.

Rows 21–24: As Rows 5-8.
Rows 25-28: With D, rep Rows 1–4.
Rows 29–32: As Rows 5-8. Rep Rows 1–32 for Body Pattern.

INSTRUCTIONS:
BACK
Beg at lower edge with color A and larger needles, cast on 77 (81, 85, 89) sts. K 1 row.
Next Row: P1; (k1, p1) across. Beg Body Pattern. Work even to approx 12½ (13, 13½, 14)" from beg, ending with a WS row.
Raglan Shaping
Bind off 2 sts at beg of next 2 rows. **Dec Row:** K1, ssk, pattern across to last 3 sts, k2tog, k1. Next Row: P2, pattern across, ending p2. Rep Dec Row every 4th row 3 (4, 5, 5) times more, then every 2nd row 17 (17, 17, 18) times, ending with a WS row. Place rem 31 (33, 35, 37) sts onto a holder.

FRONT
Work as for Back until piece measures approx 18 (19, 20,

21)" from beg, ending with a WS row and placing markers either side of center 13 (15, 17, 19) sts.
Neck Shaping
Cont Raglan Shaping, work to marker, place center 13 (15, 17, 19) sts onto a holder, join a new strand of yarn and work to end. Working sides separately and at the same time, dec 1 st each neck edge every other row 4 times. When piece measures same length as Back, ending with a WS row, place rem 5 sts for each shoulder onto safety pins.

SLEEVES (make two)
Beg at lower edge with color A and larger needles, cast on 31 (33, 35, 37) sts. Knit 1 row.
Next Row: P1; (k1, p1) across.
Body Pattern
Row 1 (RS): With B, knit.
Row 2: With B, p1; (k1, p1) across.
Rows 3–4: As Rows 1-2.
Rows 5–7: With A, knit.
Row 8: With A, p1; (k1, p1) across.
Rep Rows 1–8 for Body Pattern to approx 2" from beg, ending with a WS row.
Inc Row: K1, M1, pattern across to last st, M1, k1. Inc 1 st each edge every 4th row 3 (4, 0, 0) times more then every 6th row 9 (9, 11, 9) times and every 8th row 0 (0, 2, 4) times—57 (61, 63, 65)

sts. Cont in pattern to approx 12½ (13, 15, 16)" from beg, ending with a WS row.

Raglan Shaping
Bind off 2 sts at beg of next 2 rows. **Dec Row:** K1, ssk, pattern across to last 3 sts, k2tog, k1. Next Row: P2, pattern across, ending p2. Rep Dec Row every 4th row 7 (7, 8, 8) times more then every 2nd row 9 (11, 11, 12) times, ending with a WS row. Place rem 19 sts onto a holder.

FINISHING
Neckband
With RS facing, using smaller needle and color B, begin with back and k1, ssk, k25 (27, 29, 31) sts, k2tog. K2tog over last st from back and first st from sleeve, on sleeve, ssk, k13, k2tog. K2tog over last st from sleeve and first st from front, on front, k3tog, k1, pick up and k9 sts evenly spaced along side of neck, k13 (15, 17, 19) sts from holder, pick up and k9 sts along side of neck, k1, k3tog. K2tog over last st from front and first st from sleeve, on

sleeve, ssk, k13, k2tog. K2tog over last st from sleeve and first st from back—96 (100, 104, 108) sts. Place marker to indicate beg of rnd; join. **Rnd 1:** (P1, k1) around. **Rnds 2–5:** As Rnd 1. **Rnds 6–11:** With color C, rep Rnd 1. Bind off loosely and knitwise. Turn neckband to inside and whip st in place.

Join raglans, sides, and sleeve seams. Hide ends on WS of fabric.

winter sky pullover

photos on pages 16–17

SKILL LEVEL: Easy

SIZES: S (M, LARGE, XL, XXL)
Note: The pattern is written for the smallest size with changes for larger sizes in parentheses. When only one number is given, it applies to all sizes. For ease in working, before you begin, circle the numbers pertaining to the size you are knitting.

FINISHED MEASUREMENTS:
Chest: 40 (44, 47, 50, 54)"
Length: 27 (28, 29, 30, 31)"

MATERIALS:
Brown Sheep, Country Classic, 100% wool, worsted-weight yarn (190 yards per skein): 6 (7, 7, 8, 9) skeins of Winter Sky (R90)
Size 8 (5 mm) knitting needles or size needed to obtain gauge
Size 7 (4.5 mm) knitting needles
Size 7 (4.5 mm) circular needle, 24" length
Cable needle (cn)
Stitch marker
Yarn needle

GAUGE:
In St st with larger needles, 16 sts and 21 rows = 4"/10 cm. TAKE TIME TO CHECK YOUR GAUGE.

SPECIAL ABBREVIATIONS:
C6B: Slip 3 sts to cn and hold at back, k3, k3 from cn.
C6F: Slip 3 sts to cn and hold at front, k3, k3 from cn.

STITCHES USED:
Ribbing (a multiple of 4 sts +2 sts; a rep of 2 rows)
Row 1 (WS): P2; (k2, p2) across.
Row 2: K2; (p2, k2) across. Rep Rows 1–2 for Ribbing.

Cable Panel (over 16 sts; a rep of 10 rows)
Row 1 (WS): K2, p12, k2.
Row 2: P2, k12, p2.
Rows 3–8: Rep Rows 1–2, 3 times.
Row 9: Rep Row 1.
Row 10: P2, C6B, C6F, p2. Rep Rows 1–10 for Cable Panel.

45

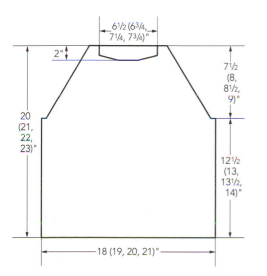

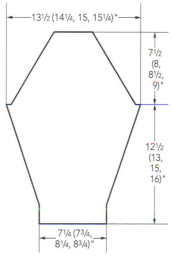

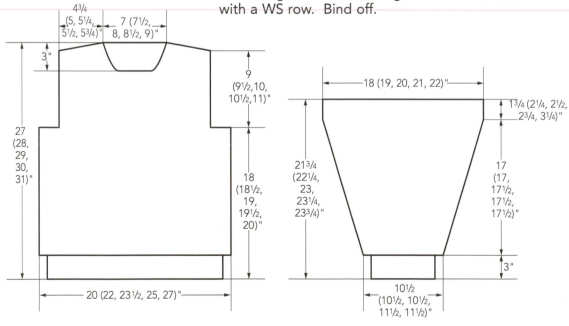

INSTRUCTIONS:
BACK
Beg at lower edge with smaller needles, cast on 78 (86, 94, 98, 106) sts. Work Ribbing to approx 3" from beg, ending with a RS row and inc 2 (2, 0, 2, 2) sts evenly across last row—80 (88, 94, 100, 108) sts. Change to larger needles and work in St st (purl WS rows, knit RS rows). Work even to approx 18 (18½, 19, 19½, 20)" from beg, ending with a RS row.

Armhole Shaping
Bind off 7 (9, 10, 11, 13) sts at beg of next 2 rows—66 (70, 74, 78, 82) sts. Work even to approx 27 (28, 29, 30, 31)" from beg, ending with a WS row.

Shoulder and Neck Shaping
Bind off 19 (20, 21, 22, 23) sts at beg of next 2 rows. Bind off rem 28 (30, 32, 34, 36) sts.

FRONT
Cast on and work Ribbing as for Back.

Set Up for Body Pattern, Row 1 (WS):
P32 (36, 39, 42, 46) sts, Cable Panel Row 1 over 16 sts, p to end. Pattern is now set. Work even to approx 18 (18½, 19, 19½, 20)" from beg, ending with a RS row.

Armhole Shaping
Work as for Back. Work even on rem 66 (70, 74, 78, 82) sts to approx 24 (25, 26, 27, 28)" from beg, ending with a WS row.

Neck Shaping
K25 (26, 27, 28, 29) sts, join a new ball of yarn and bind off center 12 (14, 16, 18, 20) sts, k to end. Working sides separately and at the same time, bind off at each neck edge 3 sts once, 2 sts once, and 1 st once. Cont on rem 19 (20, 21, 22, 23) sts to same length as Back, ending with a WS row. Bind off.

SLEEVES (make two)
Beg at lower edge with smaller needles, cast on 42 (42, 42, 46, 46) sts. Work Ribbing to approx 3" from beg, ending with a RS row. Change to larger needles and p across next row. Inc 1 st each edge NOW and every 4th row 1 (7, 12, 14, 20) times and every 6th row 13 (9, 6, 4, 0) times. Work even on 72 (76, 80, 84, 88) sts to approx 21¾ (22¼, 23, 23¼, 23¾)" from beg, ending with a WS row. Bind off.

46

FINISHING

Join shoulder seams. Set in sleeves, joining sleeve tops to bound off sts to form square armholes. Join underarm and side seams.

Neckband

With RS facing and circular needle, beg at right shoulder, pick up and k68 (72, 76, 80, 84) sts evenly spaced around neck. Place a marker to indicate beg of round. **Rnd 1:** (K2, p2) around. Rep Rnd 1 to approx 1¼" from beg. Bind off in ribbing.

colorwork turtleneck

photos on pages 18–19

SKILL LEVEL: Easy

SIZES: XS (S, MEDIUM, L, XL)
Note: The pattern is written for the smallest size with changes for larger sizes in parentheses. When only one number is given, it applies to all sizes. For ease in working, before you begin, circle the numbers pertaining to the size you are knitting.

FINISHED MEASUREMENTS:
Bust: 36 (38, 40, 42, 43½)"
Length: 18 (19, 20, 21, 22)"

MATERIALS:
Coats & Clark Red Heart, TLC Essentials, 100% acrylic, worsted-weight yarn (4½ ounces per skein): 2 (3, 3, 3, 4) skeins of Falling Leaves (2958) for A
Coats & Clark Red Heart, TLC Heathers, 100% acrylic, worsted-weight yarn (5 ounces per skein): 2 (2, 3, 3, 3) skeins of Port Wine (2495) for B
Size 8 (5 mm) knitting needles or size needed to obtain gauge
Size 6 (4 mm) knitting needles
Yarn needle

GAUGE:
In Body Pattern with larger needles, 18 sts and 22 rows = 4"/10 cm.
TAKE TIME TO CHECK YOUR GAUGE.

SPECIAL ABBREVIATIONS:
Wyif: With yarn in front.
Yb: Yarn back.
Sl1p: Slip first stitch purlwise.

STITCHES USED:
Ribbing (over 15 sts; a rep of 4 rows)
Row 1 (WS): Wyif, sl1p, p14.
Row 2: As Row 1.
Row 3: Wyif, sl1p, yb, k14.
Row 4: As Row 2.
Rep Rows 1–4 for Ribbing.

Body Pattern (a multiple of 4 sts + 2 sts; a rep of 8 rows)
Row 1 (WS): With B, knit.
Row 2: K2-B; (k2-A, k2-B) across.
Row 3: P2-B; (p2-A, p2-B) across.
Row 4: K2-A; (k2-B, k2-A) across.
Row 5: P2-A; (p2-B, p2-A) across.
Rows 6–7: Rep Rows 2-3.
Row 8: With B, knit.
Rep Rows 1–8 for Body Pattern.

NOTES: *When working with two colors in one row, carry unused strand loosely along WS of fabric. When changing color, bring new strand from under present strand for a "twist" to prevent holes.*

INSTRUCTIONS:
BACK
Ribbing
With smaller needles and A, cast on 15 sts. Work Ribbing Rows 1–4 for 40 (42, 44, 46, 48) times. Rep Row 1 again. Bind off knitwise.
Upper Body
With RS facing, using smaller needles and B, pick up and k82 (86, 90, 94, 98) sts evenly spaced along one edge of Ribbing. **Note:** It works best to pick up 1 st in each slip st

along edge with 1 st at either end. Change to larger needles and beg Body Pattern. Work even to approx 10½ (11, 11½, 12, 12½)" from beg, ending with a WS row.

Armhole Shaping
Bind off 12 sts at beg of next 2 rows. Work even on 58 (62, 66, 70, 74) sts to approx 18 (19, 20, 21, 22)" from beg, ending with a WS row.

Shoulder and Neck Shaping
Bind off 15 (16, 17, 18, 19) sts each shoulder edge once. Bind off rem 28 (30, 32, 34, 36) sts.

FRONT
Work as for Back to approx 15½ (16½, 17½, 18½, 19½)" from beg, ending with a WS row.

Neck Shaping
Pattern across first 21 (22, 23, 24, 25) sts; join new balls and bind off center 16 (18, 20, 22, 24) sts; work to end of row. Working sides separately and at the same time, bind off at each neck edge 3 sts once, 2 sts once, and 1 st once. Cont in pattern on rem 15 (16, 17, 18, 19) sts until piece measures same length

as Back, ending with a WS row. Bind off rem sts for each shoulder.

SLEEVES (make two)
Ribbing
With smaller needles and A, cast on 15 sts. Work Ribbing Rows 1–4 for 22 (22, 22, 24, 24) times. Rep Row 1 again. Bind off knitwise. With RS facing using smaller needles and B, pick up and k 46 (46, 46, 50, 50) sts evenly spaced along edge. Change to larger needles and work Rows 1–7 of Body Pattern. Including new sts into pattern as they accumulate, inc 1 st each edge NOW and every 4th row 0 (0, 4, 4, 8) times, every 6th row 1 (12, 10, 10, 8) times, and every 8th row 8 (0, 0, 0, 0) times. Work even on 66 (72, 76, 80, 84) sts to approx 21½ (21½, 22, 22½, 23)" from beg, ending with a WS row. Bind off.

FINISHING
Join shoulder seams. Set in sleeves, sewing bound off sts to sleeve sides for square armholes. Join underarm and side seams.

Neckband
With smaller needles and A, cast on 15 sts. Work Ribbing Rows 1–4 until neckband when slightly stretched fits around neck opening. Rep Row 1 and bind off. Sew short edges tog. Pin neckband around neck, placing seam at center back. Sew in place.

ocean waves top
photo on page 20

SKILL LEVEL: Easy

SIZES: XS (S, MEDIUM, L, XL)
Note: The pattern is written for the smallest size with changes for larger sizes in parentheses. When only one number is given, it applies to all sizes. For ease in working, before you begin, circle the numbers pertaining to the size you are knitting.

FINISHED MEASUREMENTS:
Bust: 38 (40, 42, 44, 46)"
Length: 22 (22½, 23, 23½, 24)"

MATERIALS:
Aurora Yarns, Muskat, 100% Egyptian cotton sport-weight yarn, (100 meters per ball): 11 (12, 13, 14, 15) balls of Taupe (61) for A, 1 (1, 1, 2, 2) ball(s) of Purple (43) for B, and 1 (1, 1, 2, 2) ball(s) of Green (25) for C
Size 4 (3.5 mm) knitting needles or size needed to obtain gauge
Two ring-type stitch markers
Tapestry needle

GAUGE:
In Body Pattern, 24 sts and 32 rows = 4"/10 cm.
TAKE TIME TO CHECK YOUR GAUGE.

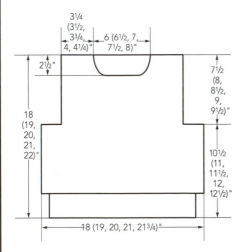

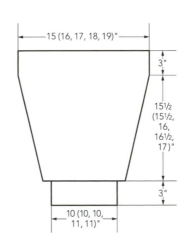

SPECIAL ABBREVIATIONS:

Sl 1 wyib: Slip next stitch purlwise and with yarn at back of fabric.

Sl 1 wyif: Slip next stitch purlwise and with yarn at front of fabric.

Sl 3 wyif: Slip next 3 stitches purlwise and with yarn at front of fabric.

Sl 2 wyib: Slip next 2 stitches purlwise and with yarn at back of fabric.

Sl 2 wyif: Slip next 2 stitches purlwise and with yarn at front of fabric.

Sl 3 wyib: Slip next 3 stitches purlwise and with yarn at back of fabric.

Sssk: Slip next 3 sts knitwise, one at a time to right-hand needle, insert tip of left-hand needle into front of these 3 sts and k them together.

Ssk: Slip next 2 sts knitwise, one at a time to right-hand needle, insert tip of left-hand needle into fronts of these 2 sts and k them together.

STITCHES USED:

Body Pattern (a multiple of 16 sts + 1 st; a rep of 10 rows)
Row 1 (RS): With A, knit.
Row 2: With A, purl.
Row 3: With A, k1; (k15, sl 1 wyib) across, ending k16.
Row 4: With A, p1, sl 1 wyif; (p13, sl 3 wyif) across, ending p13, sl 1 wyif, p1.
Row 5: With A, k1; (sl 2 wyib, k11, sl 2 wyib, k1) across.
Row 6: With A, p2; (sl 2 wyif, p9, sl 2 wyif, p3) across, ending sl 2 wyif, p9, sl 2 wyif, p2.
Row 7: With A, k3; (sl 2 wyib, k7, sl 2 wyib, k5) across, ending sl 2 wyib, k7, sl 2 wyib, k3.
Row 8: With A, p4; (sl 2 wyif, p5, sl 2 wyif, p7) across, ending sl 2 wyif, p5, sl 2 wyif, p4.

Row 9: With B, k5; (sl 2 wyib, k3, sl 2 wyib, k9) across, ending sl 2 wyib, k3, sl 2 wyib, k5.
Row 10: With B, p6; (sl 2 wyif, p1, sl 2 wyif, p11) across, ending sl 2 wyif, p1, sl 2 wyif, p6.
Rows 11–18: As Rows 1-8.
Rows 19–20: With C, rep Rows 9–10.
Rep Rows 1–20 for Body Pattern.

INSTRUCTIONS:
BACK
Beg at the lower edge with A, cast on 115 (121, 127, 131, 139) sts.
Ribbing
Row 1 (WS): P1; (k1, p1) across.
Row 2: K1; (p1, k1) across.
Rows 3–6: As Rows 1–2.
Next Row: With A, purl across. Set Up for Body Pattern: K9 (12, 15, 17, 21) sts, pm, k97, pm, k to end. Work Row 2 of Body Pattern, slipping markers. Keeping sts outside of markers in St st (knit RS rows, purl WS rows), beg with Row 3 and work even to approx 15" from beg, ending with a WS row.

Armhole Shaping
Dec 1 st each edge every row 7 (8, 9, 9, 11) times—101 (105, 109, 113, 117) sts. Cont even to approx 22 (22½, 23, 23½, 24)" from beg, ending with a WS row.
Shoulder and Neck Shaping
Bind off 7 (8, 8, 8, 9) sts each shoulder edge twice and 8 (7, 8, 9, 8) sts each shoulder edge once. Bind off rem 57 (59, 61, 63, 65) sts.

FRONT
Work as for Back until piece measures approx 17 (17½, 18, 18½, 19)" from beg, ending with a WS row.
Neck Shaping
Pattern across first 50 (52, 54, 56, 58) sts, place center st onto a safety pin, join new balls and work to end row. Work sides separately and at the same time as follows: **RS Row:** Pattern across to last 4 sts, k3tog, k1; for second side, k1, sssk, pattern to end. **WS Row:** Pattern across to last 2 sts, p2; for second side, p2, pattern to end. Rep last 2 rows for 7 (8, 9, 10, 11) times more—34 sts on each side. **Next Dec Row:** Pattern

across to last 3 sts, k2tog, k1, for second side, k1, ssk, pattern to end. **Next Row:** Pattern across to last 2 sts, p2; for second side, p2, pattern to end. Rep last 2 rows for 11 (10, 9, 8, 7) times more. Work even on rem 22 (23, 24, 25, 26) sts for each shoulder to same length as Back. Shape shoulders as for Back.

SLEEVES (make two)
Beg at lower edge with A, cast on 67 sts. Rep Ribbing Rows 1–6 as for Back. Next Row: With A, purl across. Work St st to approx 4" from beg, ending with a WS row. Inc 1 st each edge NOW and then every 14th (10th, 8th, 6th, 6th) row for 8 (11, 14, 17, 20) TOTAL times. Cont in St st on the 83 (89, 95, 101, 107) sts to approx 20" from beg, ending with a WS row.
Sleeve Cap Shaping
Dec 1 st each edge every row 7 (8, 9, 9, 11) times. On next RS row, bind off rem 69 (73, 77, 83, 85) sts.

FINISHING
Join left shoulder seam.

Neck Edging
RS facing, using A, pick up and k 57 (59, 61, 63, 65) sts along back neck, pick up and k 40 sts evenly spaced along side of neck, k1 from holder, pick up and k 40 sts evenly spaced along second side of neck. Bind off loosely and knitwise.
Join right shoulder and neck edging. Set in sleeves. Join underarm and side seams.

sunshine halter

photo on page 21

SKILL LEVEL: Intermediate

SIZES: XS (SMALL, M, L)
Note: The pattern is written for the smallest size with changes for larger sizes in parentheses. When only one number is given, it applies to all sizes. For ease in working, before you begin, circle the numbers pertaining to the size you are knitting.

FINISHED MEASUREMENTS:
Bust: 30 (33, 36, 40)"
Length: 12"

MATERIALS:
Patons, Grace, 100% cotton, sport-weight yarn (136 yards per ball): 3 (3, 3, 4) balls of Apricot (60603) for MC; 1 ball each of Ginger (60027) for color A and Fern (60527) for color B
Size 5 (3.75 mm) knitting needles or size needed to obtain gauge
Size 4 (3.5 mm) knitting needles
Cable needle (cn)
Tapestry needle

GAUGE:
In Body Pattern with larger needles, 24 sts and 32 rows = 4"/10 cm.
TAKE TIME TO CHECK YOUR GAUGE.

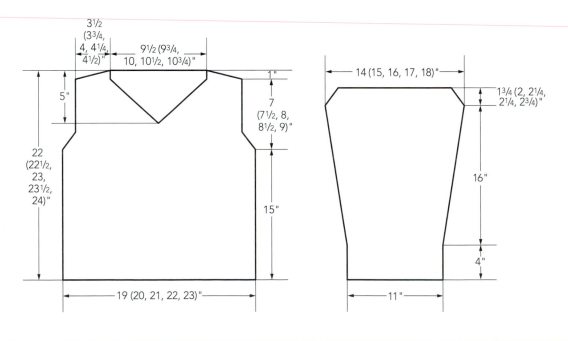

Rows 7–8: As Rows 1–2.
Rows 9–10: With B, rep Rows 3–4.
Rows 11-12: With MC, rep Rows 5–6.
Rep Rows 1–12 for Body Pattern.
After first 12 rows of **Body Pattern on next row:** K1, M1, pattern across, ending M1, k1—76 (84, 96, 106) sts. Work 7 pattern rows. Including new sts into Body Pattern as they accumulate, inc 1 st each edge as est every 8th row 7 times more— 90 (98, 110, 120) sts. Work even to approx 12" from beg, ending with Row 5 or Row 11. With MC, knit across next row for Fold Line. Change to smaller needles and work 10 rows of St st, beg with a knit row. Bind off knitwise on RS.

FRONT
As for Back.

STRAPS (make two)
With smaller needles and MC, cast on 9 sts.
Row 1 (RS): K2; (p1, k1) 3 times, k1.
Row 2: (K1, p1) 4 times, k1.
Rep Rows 1–2 until strap measures approx 19" from beg. Bind off.

FINISHING
Sew side seams. With the WS facing, turn hems to inside along Fold Line and sew in place. Place markers 3½" from each edge along top of front matching pattern as shown. Beginning at the marker, sew each strap in place.

SPECIAL ABBREVIATIONS:
M1: Lift running thread before next stitch onto left-hand needle and knit in its back loop to make one stitch.
PW2: Purl, wrapping yarn around needle twice.
Tw4B: Slip next 2 sts onto cn and hold at back of work. Slip next 2 sts onto right-hand needle purlwise and drop extra loops, k2 from cn.
Tw4F: Dropping extra loops slip next 2 sts purlwise onto cn and hold at front of work. K2 from cn, slip sts from cn back onto right-hand needle.
Sl 2: Slip next 2 sts to right-hand needle, purlwise and with yarn on WS of fabric.

INSTRUCTIONS:
BACK
Beg at lower edge with smaller needles and MC, cast on 74 (82, 94, 104) sts. Beg with a knit row, work 11 St st rows (knit RS rows, purl WS rows). Fold Line: Knit. Change to larger needles.

Body Pattern
Row 1 (RS): With MC, knit.
Row 2: With MC, p2 (6, 5, 3); * p5, (PW2) 4 times, p5; rep from * across, ending p2 (6, 5, 3).
Row 3: With A, k2 (6, 5, 3); *k3, Tw4B, Tw4F, k3; rep from * across, ending k2 (6, 5, 3).
Row 4: With A, p2 (6, 5, 3); *p3, sl 2, p4, sl 2, p3; rep from * across, ending p2 (6, 5, 3).
Row 5: With MC, knit.
Row 6: With MC, purl

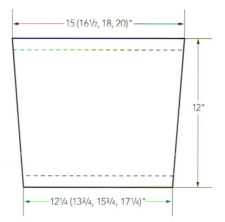

15 (16½, 18, 20)"

12"

12¼ (13¾, 15¾, 17¼)"

orange peel sweater

photos on pages 22–23

SKILL LEVEL: Easy

SIZES: S (MEDIUM, L, XL)
Note: The pattern is written for the smallest size with changes for larger sizes in parentheses. When only one number is given, it applies to all sizes. For ease in working, before you begin, circle the numbers pertaining to the size you are knitting.

FINISHED MEASUREMENTS:
Bust: 32 (36, 40, 44)"
Length: 21 (21½, 22, 22½)"

MATERIALS:
Classic Elite, Bravo, 40% rayon/35% mohair/13% silk/6% wool/6% nylon, bulky-weight yarn (48 yards per hank): 6 (7, 7, 8) hanks of orange (3727)

Size 11 (8 mm) circular needles, 16" and 29" lengths, or size needed to obtain gauge
Two ring-type stitch markers

GAUGE:
In St st rnds (knit every rnd), 12 sts and 16 rnds = 4"/10 cm.
TAKE TIME TO CHECK YOUR GAUGE.

SPECIAL ABBREVIATIONS:
Rdec (Right Decrease): K1, slip this stitch back to left-hand needle, pass 2nd stitch over k1 and return to right-hand needle
Ldec (Left Decrease): Slip one stitch purlwise and with yarn on WS of fabric, k1, pass the slipped stitch over the k1
K-Inc (Knit Increase): Knit in front and back of next stitch

STITCHES USED:
Spiral Rib (a multiple of 3 sts; a rep of 3 rnds)
Rnd 1: (K2, p1) around.
Rnd 2: (P1, k2) around.
Rnd 3: (K1, p1, k1) around.
Rep Rnds 1–3 for Spiral Rib.

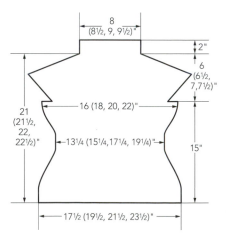

Note: This sweater is worked in rounds (rnds) on a circular needle. After the lower border is worked, knit every rnd for St st to the underarm shaping.

INSTRUCTIONS:
BODY
Beg at the lower edge with longer needle, cast on 105 (117, 129, 141) sts. Making sure not to twist the sts, join in circle and pm to indicate beg of rnd. Work Spiral Rib pattern for 6 rnds, decreasing 1 st on last rnd—104 (116, 128, 140) sts. **Next Rnd:** Slip marker (first side seam), k52 (58, 64, 70) sts, pm (2nd side seam), k52 (58, 64, 70) sts. **Dec Rnd:** (K1, Rdec, k to within 4 sts of marker, Ldec, k2, slip marker) twice. Rep Dec Rnd every 6th rnd 5 times more—80 (92, 104, 116) sts. K 8 rnds even. **Inc Rnd:** * K1, inc in next st, k to within 3 sts of marker, inc in next st, k2; rep from * again. Rep Inc Rnd every 4th rnd 3 times more—96 (108, 120, 132) sts. Work even to approx 15" from beg. Next Rnd: K to within 3 (4, 5, 6) sts of beg rnd marker.
Armhole Shaping
Removing markers, bind off 6 (8, 10, 11) sts, k41 (45, 49, 54) MORE sts—42 (46, 50, 55) sts each for front and back, bind off 6 (8, 10, 11) sts, k to end of rnd.

SLEEVES
At bind-off "hole", pm, cast on 27 (30, 33, 36) sts for sleeve, pm, k42 (46, 50, 55), pm, cast on 27 (30, 33, 36) for sleeve, pm, k42 (46, 50, 55)—138 (152,166,182) sts. **Next 5 Rnds:** Work Spiral Rib pattern on the 27 (30, 33, 36)

52

sleeve sts between the markers and keep 42 (46, 50, 55) front/back stitches in St st. Continue in St st until sleeve measures approx 1½ (1½, 2, 2½)", dec 2 (0, 2, 2) sts on last rnd—136 (152, 164, 180) sts.

YOKE

Rnd 1: (K2, k2tog) around—102 (114, 123, 135) sts.
Rnd 2: (K2, p1) around.
Rnds 3–5: Knit.
Rnd 6: K around, dec 2 (2, 3, 3) sts evenly—100 (112, 120, 132) sts.
Rnd 7: Rep Rnd 1—75 (84, 90, 99) sts.
Rnd 8: Rep Rnd 2.
Rnds 9–11: Knit.
Rnd 12: K around and dec 3 (0, 2, 3) sts evenly spaced—72 (84, 88, 96) sts.
Change to shorter needle.
Rnd 13: Rep Rnd 1—54 (63, 66, 72) sts.
Rnd 14: Rep Rnd 2.
Rnds 15–17: Knit.
Rnd 18: K around and dec 6 (12, 12, 15) sts evenly spaced—48 (51, 54, 57) sts.
Rnd 19: Rep Rnd 2.
Rnd 20: Knit.

reversible tweed scarf

For Neck Border, begin with Rnd 3 of Spiral Rib; then rep Rnds 1–3 twice, and then Rnd 1 again. Bind off loosely purlwise.

reversible tweed scarf

photos on pages 24–25

SKILL LEVEL: Easy

SIZE: 8 × 80"

MATERIALS:
Patons, Shetland Chunky, 75% acrylic/25% wool, chunky-weight yarn (148 yards per ball): 2 balls each of Deep Plum (03405) and High Plains Variegated (03609)
Size 13 (9 mm) knitting needles or size needed to obtain gauge

GAUGE:
In Body Pattern using 2 strands of yarn, 10 sts and 14 rows = 4"/10 cm. TAKE TIME TO CHECK YOUR GAUGE.

STITCHES USED:
 Body Pattern (a multiple of 3 sts + 2 sts; a rep of 4 rows)
  Row 1 (RS): (K2, p1) across, ending k2.

quick and easy scarf

Row 2: (P2, k1) across, ending p2.
Row 3: As Row 1.
Row 4 (WS): Knit.
Rep Rows 1–4 for Body Pattern.

INSTRUCTIONS:
With 1 strand of each color, cast on 20 sts. Work in Body Pattern to approx 80" from beg, ending with Row 3. Bind off.

quick-and-easy scarf

photos on pages 24–25

SKILL LEVEL: Easy

SIZE: Approximately 8 × 62", excluding fringe

MATERIALS:
Coats & Clark Red Heart Light & Lofty, 100% acrylic, bulky-weight yarn (6 ounces per skein): 1 skein each of Puff (9316) for A and Café Au Lait (9334) for B
Size 15 (10 mm) knitting needles or size needed to obtain gauge
Size N/15 (10 mm) crochet hook

GAUGE:
In Pattern, 10 sts and 12 rows = 4"/10 cm. TAKE TIME TO CHECK YOUR GAUGE.

SPECIAL ABBREVIATION:
Sl 2-p: With yarn on WS of fabric, slip next 2 stitches purlwise.

INSTRUCTIONS:
With A, cast on 20 sts.
Row 1 (WS): With A, purl.
Row 2: With B, k1; (sl 2-p, k4) across, ending k1.
Row 3: With B, k1; (p4, sl 2-p) across, ending k1.
Row 4: With A, k1; (k4, sl 2-p) across, ending k1.
Row 5: With A, k1; (sl 2-p, p4) across, ending k1.
Row 6: With B, k3; (sl 2-p, k4) across to last 5 sts, sl 2-p, k3.
Row 7: With B, k1, p2; (sl 2-p, p4) across to last 5 sts, sl 2-p, p2, k1.
Rows 8–9: With A, rep Rows 2–3.
Rows 10–11: With B, rep Rows 4–5.
Rows 12–13: With A, rep Rows 6–7.
Rep Rows 2–13 for pattern until piece measures approx 62" from beg, ending with Row 5 or Row 11. With A, bind off loosely and knitwise.

Fringe
Cut 2 strands of A measuring approx 24" long. Holding strands tog, fold in half to form a loop. With WS of scarf facing and crochet hook, take loop through first stitch at right edge. Take ends through loop and pull up to form a knot. Add 11 fringe to each end. Trim ends.

kaleidoscope raglan

photos on pages 26–27

SKILL LEVEL: Easy

SIZES: XS (S, MEDIUM, L, XL)
Note: The pattern is written for the smallest size with changes for larger sizes in parentheses. When only one number is given, it applies to all sizes. For ease in working, before you begin, circle the numbers pertaining to the size you are knitting.

FINISHED MEASUREMENTS:
Bust: 33 (34½, 36, 38, 41)"
Length (including border): 15¾ (16½, 17, 17½, 18)"

MATERIALS:
Muench Yarns, Sierra, 77% wool/23% nylon, bulky-weight yarn (50 grams per ball):
9 (10, 11, 12, 13) balls of Blue/Purple Multi (G153-003)
Size 13 (9 mm) knitting needles or size needed to obtain gauge
Size 11 (8 mm) circular knitting needle, 16" length
Four stitch holders
Yarn needle

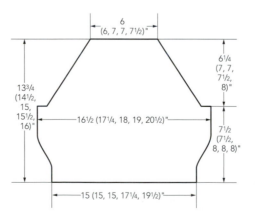

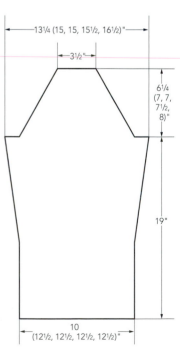

GAUGE:

In St st (knit RS rows, purl WS rows) with larger needles, 10 sts and 14 rows = 4"/10 cm. TAKE TIME TO CHECK YOUR GAUGE.

SPECIAL ABBREVIATIONS:

Ssk: Slip next 2 sts knitwise one at a time to right-hand needle, insert tip of left needle into fronts of these 2 sts and k them together.

Notes: Borders along lower edges add an additional 2", unreflected on the diagrams. For ease in working the borders, turn only the garter-stitch portion.

INSTRUCTIONS:
BACK

Beg at lower edge and above border, with larger needles cast on 37 (37, 37, 43, 49) sts. Beg with a purl row work 5 St st rows. **Inc Row (RS):** Inc 1 st each edge. Work 3 St st rows. Rep last 4 rows 1 (2, 3, 1, 0) times more—41 (43, 45, 47, 51) sts. Work even to approx 7½ (7½, 8, 8, 8)" from beg, ending with a WS row.
Raglan Shaping
Bind off 3 sts at beg of next 2 rows. **Dec Row:** K2, ssk, k across, ending k2tog, k2. Purl next row. Rep last 2 rows for 9 (10, 10, 11, 12) times more, ending with a WS row. Place rem 15 (15, 17, 17, 19) sts onto a holder.
Border
With RS facing and larger needles, pick up and k36 (36, 36, 42, 48) sts evenly spaced along lower edge. Knit across for Garter St. With circular needle, (k4; turn) 12 times. * Bind off 6 sts, k 3 additional sts

(4 sts); (k4; turn) 11 times. Rep from * across, ending last rep with bind off 5 sts and fasten off.

FRONT
As for Back.

SLEEVES (make two)
Beg at lower edge and above border, with larger needles cast on 25 (31, 31, 31, 31) sts. Beg with a purl row work St st to approx 6 (8, 8, 8, 6)" from beg. **Inc Row:** Inc 1 st each edge. Work 9 St st rows. Rep last 10 rows 4 (2, 2, 3, 4) times more—35 (37, 37, 39, 41) sts. Work even to approx 19" from beg, ending with a WS row.
Raglan Shaping
Work as for Back. Place rem 9 sts onto holder.
Border
Work as for Back.

FINISHING
Neck Border
With circular needle, k9 sleeve sts, k15 (15, 17, 17, 19) sts from front, k9 sleeve sts, k15 (15, 17, 17, 19) sts from back—48 (48, 52, 52, 56) sts. Bind off knitwise on WS of fabric.

Join raglan sleeves to front and back. Join underarm and side seams, leaving borders free.

all-american dress and hat

photos on pages 28–29

SIZES:
Dress: 2T (THREE TODDLER, 4T)
Note: The pattern is written for the smallest size with changes for larger sizes in parentheses. When only one number is given, it applies to all sizes. For ease in working, before you begin, circle the numbers pertaining to the size you are knitting.

FINISHED MEASUREMENTS:
Chest: 19 (22½, 23½)"
Length: 15½ (17, 19)"

MATERIALS:
Classic Elite, Provence, 100% cotton, DK-weight yarn (256 yards per hank):
Dress: 1 (1, 2) hank(s) Red (2658); 1 hank each of Blue (2657) and White (2601).
Hat: 1 hank each of Red (2658), Blue (2657) and

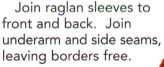

White (2601). *Note: There is enough blue and white in one hank for the hat and the dress.*
Size 8 (5 mm) knitting needles or size needed to obtain gauge
2 stitch holders
Yarn needle

GAUGE:
In St st (knit RS rows, purl WS rows), 18 sts and 22 rows = 4"/10 cm.
TAKE TIME TO CHECK YOUR GAUGE

SPECIAL ABBREVIATIONS:
Sl1, k1, psso: Slip next stitch purlwise and with yarn on WS, knit 1 stitch, pass the slipped stitch over the k1.

INSTRUCTIONS FOR DRESS:
BACK
With blue cast on 79 (91, 94) sts. K 4 rows for Garter St border. Purl next row. Next Row: K1; (k2tog, k1) across—53 (61, 63) sts. Knit next row. Next Row: Change to red and knit across. Purl next row. Work 8 more St st rows.
Dec Row: K2, sl1, k1, psso, k to last 4 sts, k2tog, k2—51 (59, 61) sts. Cont St st and rep Dec Row every 8th (10th, 10th) row until 43 (51, 53) sts

rem. AT THE SAME TIME, after 14 total red rows have been completed, work stripe pattern as follows: (2 rows white, 2 rows red) 3 times, 2 rows white. Work with red for remainder of dress Cont as set to approx 10 (11¼, 13)" from beg, ending with a WS row.
Armhole Shaping
Bind off 4 (5, 5) sts beg next 2 rows—35 (41, 43) sts. **Dec Row (RS):** K2, sl1, k1, psso, k to last 4 sts, k2tog, k2. Next Row: Purl across. Rep last 2 rows twice more—29 (35, 37) sts.
Neck Shaping
K7 (9, 9), k2tog, k2, bind off 7 (9, 11), with 1 st on right needle k1, sl1, k1, psso, k7 (9, 9) sts.
Right Shoulder, Row 2: P6 (8, 8), p2tog, p2—9 (11, 11) sts.
Row 3: K 2, sl1, k1, psso, k1 (3, 3), k2tog, k2—7 (9, 9) sts.
Row 4 and alternate rows: Purl across.
Row 5: K2, sl1, k1, psso, k to end—6 (8, 8) sts. For size 2T only, go to Row 9.
Row 7: K2, sl1, k1, psso, k2tog, k2— (6, 6) sts.
Row 9: K2, sl1, k1, psso, k2—5 sts.
Row 10: Purl across. Put 5 rem sts on stitch holder.
Left Shoulder: With WS facing, join yarn; p2, p2tog, p across—9 (11, 11) sts.
Row 2: K2, sl1, k1, psso, k1 (3, 3), k2tog, k2—7 (9, 9) sts.
Row 3 and alternate rows: Purl across.
Row 4: K to last 4 sts, k2tog, k2—6 (8, 8) sts. For size 2T only, go to Row 8.

Row 6: K2, sl1, k1, psso, k2tog, k2—(6, 6) sts.
Row 8: K2, k2tog, k2—5 sts.
Row 9: Purl across. Put 5 rem sts on stitch holder.

FRONT
As for Back.

FINISHING
With RS tog and yarn needle, join sides. Turn RS out. To close gap at right front neck, with yarn needle, thread end of joined yarn through first cast off st from front of st; then through first st to right from back of st. Weave end into back of shoulder strap.
Shoulder Ties (make 4)
Cut 3—24" lengths of blue yarn. With yarn needle thread yarn through one group of 5 sts on st holder. With 6 lengths even, divide in 3 and braid to end. Tie a knot 1" from end and trim ends. Weave all loose ends into WS of work.

HAT (approx 14" around)
With blue, cast on 93 sts.
K 2 rows.
Row 3: Purl across.
Row 4: Knit across.
Row 5: Purl across.
Row 6: (K1, k2tog) across—62 sts.
Row 7: Knit across. With red, cont in St st for 6 rows, beg with a knit row. Cont in St st, work 2 rows white, 2 rows red, 2 rows white, 6 rows red.
Crown Shaping
Row 1 (RS): Cont in red, k9, k2tog, (k8, k2tog) 5 times, k1—56 sts.
Row 2 and all alternate rows: Purl across.
Row 3: K8, k2tog, (k7, k2tog) 5 times, k1—50 sts.

56

Row 5: K7, k2tog, (k6, k2tog) 5 times, k1—44 sts. Cont as set, dec 6 sts on RS rows until 8 sts remain and ending with a knit row. Cut 6" tail of yarn and thread it through 8 sts on needle; gather sts and secure on WS.

FINISHING
Sew center back seam. Weave all loose ends into inside of work.

too-cute cowl neck

photos on pages 30–31

SKILL LEVEL: Easy

SIZES: S (MEDIUM, L, XL)
Note: The pattern is written for the smallest size with changes for larger sizes in parentheses. When only one number is given, it applies to all sizes. For ease in working, before you begin, circle the numbers pertaining to the size you are knitting.

FINISHED MEASUREMENTS:
Bust: 36 (40, 44, 48)"
Length: 21½ (22, 22½, 23)"

MATERIALS:
Classic Elite Yarns, Bazic Wool, 100% wool, worsted weight yarn (65 yards per hank): 13 (14, 16, 17) hanks of Aqua (2972)
Size 9 (5.5 mm) straight knitting needles or size needed to obtain gauge
Size 8 (5 mm), size 10 (6 mm), and size 10½ (6.5 mm) circular knitting needle, 16" length
Two stitch holders

Ring-type stitch markers
Yarn needle

GAUGE:
In Stockinette Stitch (St st) with straight needles, 16 sts and 17 rows = 4"/10 cm.
TAKE TIME TO CHECK YOUR GAUGE.

SPECIAL ABBREVIATIONS:
Ssk: Slip next 2 sts knitwise one at a time to right-hand needle, insert tip of left-hand needle into fronts of these 2 sts and k them together.
M1: Lift running thread before next st onto left-hand needle and knit in its back loop to make one stitch.

INSTRUCTIONS:
BACK
Beg at the lower edge with straight needles, cast on 72 (80, 88, 96) sts.
Knit 6 rows for Garter st band. Beg with a knit row, work St st (knit RS rows, purl WS rows) for 8 rows.
Dec Row (RS): K1, ssk, k across to last 3 sts, k2tog, k1. Rep Dec Row every 8th row, twice more—66 (74, 82, 90) sts. Work 7 rows even.
Inc Row (RS): K1, M1, k across to last st, M1, k1. Rep Inc Row every 8th row, twice more—72 (80, 88, 96) sts. Work even to approx 14" from beg, ending with a WS row.
Armhole Shaping
Bind off 6 (7, 7, 9) sts at beg of next 2 rows. **Dec Row (RS):** K2, k2tog, k across to last 4 sts, ssk, k2. Rep Dec Row every other row 10 (12, 13, 14) times more—38 (40, 46, 48) sts. Continue even to approx 21½ (22, 22½, 23)" from beg ending with a WS row.
Shoulder and Neck Shaping
Bind off 6 (6, 8, 8) sts each shoulder edge once. Place rem 26 (28, 30, 32) sts onto a holder for back neck.

FRONT
Work as for Back to approx 16½ (16½, 17, 17½)" from beg, ending with a WS row. Place markers either side of center 12 (14, 14, 16) sts.
Neck Shaping
Continue armhole shaping and work to first marker, place center 12 (14, 14, 16) sts onto a holder, join a new ball of yarn and work to end of row. Working sides separately and at the same time, dec 1 st each neck edge every row 7 (7, 8, 8) times. Continue even on rem 6 (6, 8, 8) sts for each shoulder to same length as Back, ending with a WS row. Bind off.

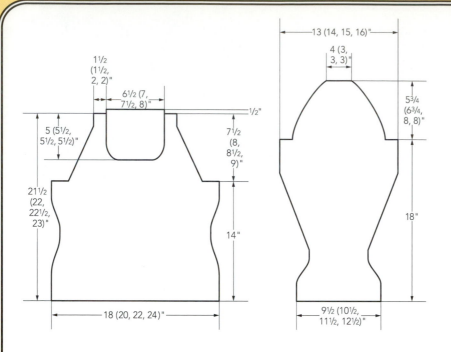

SLEEVES (make two)
Beg at the lower edge with straight needles, cast on 38 (42, 46, 50) sts. Knit 4 rows for Garter st band. Beg with a knit row, work 6 rows St st. **Dec Row (RS):** K1, k2tog, k across to last 3 sts, ssk, k1. Rep Dec Row every 4th row twice more—32 (36, 40, 44) sts. Work 7 St st rows. **Inc Row (RS):** K1, M1, k across to last st, M1, k1. Rep Inc Row every 4th row 9 times more—52 (56, 60, 64) sts. Work even to approx 18" from beg ending with a WS row.
Sleeve Cap Shaping
Bind off 6 (7, 7, 9) sts at beg of next 2 rows. **Dec Row (RS):** K2, k2tog, k across to last 4 sts, ssk, k2. Rep Dec Row every other row 9 (11, 14, 14) times more. Bind off 2 (3, 2, 2) sts beg next 2 rows. Bind off rem 16 (12, 12, 12) sts.

FINISHING
Block pieces to measurements. Join shoulder seams. Set in sleeves. Join underarm and side seams.
Cowl Neck
With the WS facing and size 8 circular needle, k26 (28, 30, 32) sts from back neck holder. Pick up and k20 (22, 22, 22) sts evenly along side of neck, k12 (14, 14, 16) sts from front holder. Pick up and k20 (22, 22, 22) sts evenly along side of neck—78 (86, 88, 92) sts. Place a marker to indicate beg of rnd; join. K 5 rnds. Change to size 10 needle; k 20 rnds. Change to size 10½ needle; continue knitting every rnd until collar measures approx 9". P 1 rnd, k 1 rnd, p 1 rnd for Garter st band. Bind off loosely and knitwise.

cotton candy jacket & booties

photos on pages 32–33

SKILL LEVEL: Easy

SIZES: Newborn (SIX MONTHS, 12 months); Booties are for size Newborn and 6 months only.
Note: *The pattern is written for the smallest size with changes for larger sizes in parentheses. When only one number is given, it applies to all sizes. For ease in working, before you begin, circle the numbers pertaining to the size you are knitting.*

FINISHED MEASUREMENTS:
Jacket Chest: 20 (24, 27½)"
Jacket Length: 9 (11, 13)"
Booties Length: 3 (3¾)"

MATERIALS:
Lion Brand, Lion Bouclé, 79% acrylic/20% mohair/1% nylon, bulky-weight yarn (57 yards per ball):
Baby Jacket: 3 (3, 5) balls Sprinkles (201); Booties: 1 ball Sprinkles (201)
Size 11 (8 mm) knitting needles or size needed to obtain gauge; 2 stitch markers
Yarn needle; 2 stitch holders
One, 1"-diameter button
Crochet hook (optional) for tassel on hood

GAUGE:
In Garter St (knit every row), 7 sts and 6 ridges = 3"/7.5 cm.
TAKE TIME TO CHECK YOUR GAUGE.

Note: The jacket and booties are each worked in one piece. There is no buttonhole on the jacket; the fabric is loose enough to push the button through.

INSTRUCTIONS:
JACKET BACK
Beg at lower edge, cast on 24 (28, 32) sts. Work in Garter St to approx 5 (6, 7½)" from beg.

SLEEVES
Cont in Garter St, cast on 9 (12, 14) sts at beg of next 2 rows—42 (52, 60) sts. Work even to approx 9 (11, 13)" from beg.

RIGHT FRONT
K15 (19, 22) sts; place center 12 (14, 16) sts onto a st holder for back neck; place rem 15 (19, 22) sts onto another st holder; turn.

At neck edge, cast on 6 (7, 9) sts and knit across all sts. Cont in Garter St on 21 (26, 31) sts until sleeve measures approx 8 (10, 11)" from cast-on row, ending at sleeve edge. **Next Row:** Bind off 9 (12, 14) sts. Cont on 12 (14, 17) sts until front measures approx 5 (6, 7)" from bound-off edge of sleeve. Bind off.

LEFT FRONT
Skip center 12 (14, 16) sts, cast on 6 (7, 9) sts, k across 15 (19, 22) sts from second st holder. Complete as for Right Front.

HOOD
With RS facing, pick up and k6 (7, 9) sts evenly spaced along right front neck edge. K across 12 (14, 16) sts from back neck holder, pick up and k6 (7, 9) sts evenly spaced along left front neck edge—24 (28, 34) sts.

Hood Shaping
K 8 (10, 13), [(knit in front and back of next st—inc made), k3] twice, inc, k to end. Cont on 27 (31, 37) sts until hood measures approx 14 (17, 20)" from pick-up row. Bind off.

FINISHING
Join underarms, sides, and hood seams.

Sew center of button ¾" from edge and 5½ (7, 8½)" from base of jacket.

Optional Tassel
Cut 6—12" lengths of yarn. Tie knot one inch from each

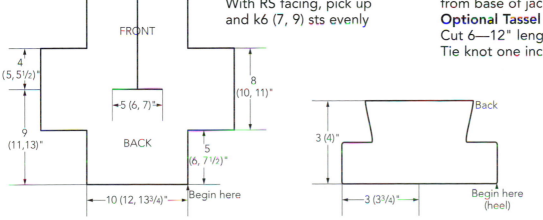

end to prevent fraying, pull knot tight. With crochet hook, pull 6 strands of yarn through outside top back corner of hood; wind 12 even lengths together tightly and make one knot as close to hood as possible, pull knot tight. Trim ends.

BOOTIES (make two)
Beg at the heel, cast on 14 (18) sts. Work in Garter St to approx 1½ (2)" from beg. **Next Row:** Bind off 3 (4) sts, at beg and end of row—8 (10) sts; turn. Join yarn, [k2 (3), inc] twice, k to end. **For Back:** Cont on 10 (12) sts to approx 3 (4)" from beg of work. Bind off.

FINISHING
Fold bootie in half at cast-on row for heel; sew from heel around to top of foot, leaving bind-off edge of Back free.
Laces (make two)
Cut 3 yards of yarn. Knot 2 ends together. Loop other end around small doorknob. Insert pencil between 2 strands at knotted end, pull tight, twist pencil to wind yarn. When yarn is tightly wound, remove pencil. Fold twisted yarn in half and remove from doorknob. Make another knot at knotted end; trim. Thread unknotted end of lace around ankle of bootie from front; knot end and trim.

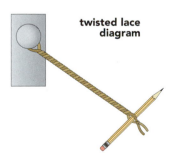

twisted lace diagram

true colors zip-up

photos on pages 34–35

SKILL LEVEL: Intermediate

SIZES: EXTRA-SMALL (S, M, L)

Note: The pattern is written for the smallest size with changes for larger sizes in parentheses. When only one number is given, it applies to all sizes. For ease in working, before you begin, circle the numbers pertaining to the size you are knitting.

FINISHED MEASUREMENTS:
Bust (zipped): 32½ (35, 39½, 45)"
Length: 19½ (20½, 21½, 22)"

MATERIALS:
Patons, Look at Me, 60% acrylic/40% nylon, sport weight (150 yards per ball): 7 (8, 8, 9) balls of Sunny Yellow (6366) for MC
Patons, Melody, 68% acrylic/32% nylon, bulky weight yarn (85 yards per ball): 3 (3, 4, 4) balls of Happy Days Variegated (9713) for A
Size 15 (10 mm) knitting needles or size needed to obtain gauge
Size 13 (9 mm) knitting needles
3 stitch holders
Separating zipper, 18 (18, 20, 20)" length
Yarn needle; sewing needle
Matching thread

GAUGE:
In St st (knit RS rows, purl WS rows), with larger needles and 3 strands of MC, 10 sts and 12 rows = 4"/10 cm.
In Rib Pattern with 1 strand of A and smaller needles, 9½ sts and 15 rows = 4"/10 cm.
TAKE TIME TO CHECK YOUR GAUGE.

SPECIAL ABBREVIATIONS:
K1B: Knit into next st, one row below, at same time, slip off st above.
M1: Lift running thread before next stitch onto left-hand needle and knit in its back loop to make one stitch.

Sl1, k1, psso: Slip next stitch purlwise and with yarn on WS, knit 1 stitch, pass the slipped stitch over the k1.
P2tog-b: Turn work slightly, insert needle from left to right into back loops of 2nd and first sts, p these two sts tog.

PATTERN STITCHES:
Rib Pattern (a multiple of 2 sts + 1 st; a rep of 2 rows)
Row 1 (RS): Knit.
Row 2: P1; (k1B, k1B, p1) across.
Rep Rows 1–2 for Rib Pattern.

NOTES: Body of jacket is worked in St st with 3 strands of MC held tog.

INSTRUCTIONS:
BACK
Beg at lower edge with smaller needles and A, cast on 31 (35, 41, 45) sts. Work Rib Pattern to approx 5" from beg, ending with a WS row and inc 2 (2, 2, 4) sts evenly spaced across last row—33 (37, 43, 49) sts. Change to larger needles.

Body
Next Row: With 3 strands of MC, k1 row, p1 row. **Inc Row:** K1, M1, k across, ending M1, k1. Work 5 rows even. Rep last 6 rows twice more—39 (43, 49, 55) sts. Work even to approx 12 (12½, 13, 13)" from beg, ending with a WS row.
Armhole Shaping
Bind off 2 (2, 3, 3) sts beg next 2 rows—35 (39, 43, 49) sts. **Dec Row (RS):** K2, k2tog, k across, ending sl1, k1, psso, k2. **Next Row:** Purl. Rep last 2 rows 1 (2, 4, 6) time(s) more—31 (33, 33, 35) sts. Work even to approx 19 (20, 21, 21½)" from beg, ending with a WS row.
Shoulder and Neck Shaping,
For Right Shoulder: k7 (8, 8, 9), k2tog; turn. Next Row: P2tog, p to end. Bind off rem 7 (8, 8, 9) sts. With RS facing, slip center 13 sts onto a holder. For Left Shoulder, join 3 strands of MC and work as follows: Sl1, k1, psso, k to end row. Next Row: P to last 2 sts, p2tog. Bind off rem 7 (8, 8, 9) sts.

RIGHT FRONT
** Beg at lower edge with smaller needles and A, cast on 17 (19, 21, 25) sts. Work Rib Pattern to approx 5" from beg, ending with a WS row and inc 1 st at center of last row—18 (20, 22, 26) sts. Change to larger needles. **
Body
Next Row: With 3 strands of MC, k across, ending M1, k1. Work 5 rows even. Rep last 6 rows twice more—21 (23, 25, 29) sts. Work even to approx 12 (12½, 13, 13)" from beg, ending with a WS row.
Armhole Shaping
Bind off 2 (2, 3, 3) sts beg next row—19 (21, 22, 26) sts.
Dec Row (RS): K across, ending sl1, k1, psso, k2.
Next Row: Purl. Rep last 2 rows 1 (2, 4, 6) time(s) more—17 (18, 17, 19) sts. Work even to approx 17 (18, 19, 19½)" from beg, ending with a RS row.
Neck Shaping
Purl to last 6 sts, p2tog, place next 4 sts onto a st holder;

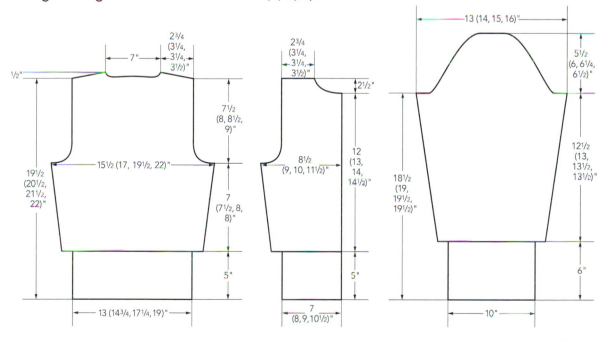

turn. **Row 1:** K2tog, k to end row. **Row 2:** Purl across, ending p2tog. Rep last 2 rows until 7 (8, 8, 9) sts rem. Work even to same length as Back, ending with a WS row. Bind off.

LEFT FRONT
Rep from ** to ** of Right Front.
Body
Next Row: With 3 strands of MC, k1, M1, k to end row. Work 5 rows even. Rep last 6 rows twice more—21 (23, 25, 29) sts. Work even to approx 12 (12½, 13, 13)" from beg, ending with a RS row.
Armhole Shaping
Bind off 2 (2, 3, 3) sts beg next row—19 (21, 22, 26) sts. **Dec Row (RS):** K2, k2tog, k to end row. **Next Row:** Purl. Rep last 2 rows 1 (2, 4, 6) time(s) more—17 (18, 17, 19) sts. Work even to approx 17 (18, 19, 19½)" from beg, ending with a RS row.
Neck Shaping
Place first 4 sts onto a holder, join 3 strands of MC. **Row 1 (WS):** P2tog, p to end row. **Row 2:** K across, ending k2tog. Rep last 2 rows until 7 (8, 8, 9) sts rem. Complete as for Right Front.

SLEEVES (make two)
Beg at lower edge with smaller needles and A, cast on 23 sts. Work Rib Pattern to approx 6" from beg, ending with a WS row and inc 2 sts on last row—25 sts. Change to larger needles and 3 strands of MC. K across next row, inc 1 st each edge. Inc 1 st each edge every 4th row 0 (0, 0, 4) times, every 6th row 0 (1, 5, 3) times, and every 8th row 3 (3, 0, 0) times. Work even on 33 (35,

37, 41) sts to approx 18½ (19, 19½, 19½)" from beg, ending with a WS row.
Sleeve Cap Shaping
Bind off 2 (2, 3, 3) sts beg next 2 rows—29 (31, 31, 35) sts. **Dec Row 1 (RS):** K2, k2tog, k across, ending sl1, k1, psso, k2. **Next Row:** Purl. Rep last 2 rows 2 (3, 4, 3) times more—23 (23, 21, 27) sts. **Dec Row 2 (RS):** K2, k2tog, k across, ending sl 1, k1, psso, k2. **Dec Row 3:** P2, p2tog-b, p across, ending p2tog, p2. Rep last 2 rows until 7 sts rem. On next RS row, bind off 7 sts.

HOOD
Sew shoulder seams. With RS facing, using smaller needles and A, k4 from right front holder, pick up and k9 sts along front neck edge and 3 sts down back neck edge. K13 from back holder, inc 2 sts evenly spaced, pick up and k3 up back neck edge and 9 along front neck edge. K4 from left front holder—47 sts.
Left Side of Hood
Row 1: P5; turn. **Row 2 and each following RS row:** Sl1 st knitwise and with yarn on WS, k to end row. **Row 3:** P6; turn. **Row 5:** P7; turn. **Row 7:** P8; turn. **Row 9:** P9; turn. **Row 11:** P10; turn. **Row 13:** P11; turn. **Row 15:** P12; turn. **Row 17:** P13; leaving a tail to weave in later, cut yarn.

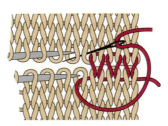

grafting diagram

Right Side of Hood
With RS facing using smaller needles, join A at right side of neck opening, k5; turn. **Row 2 and each following WS row:** Sl 1 st purlwise and with yarn on WS, p to end row. **Row 3:** K6; turn. **Row 5:** K7; turn. **Row 7:** K8; turn. **Row 9:** K9; turn. **Row 11:** K10; turn. **Row 13:** K11; turn. **Row 15:** K12; turn. **Row 17:** Knit across all 47 sts.
Beg with a purl row, work 7 St st rows. **Next Row:** K23, M1, pm, k1, pm, M1, k23. Work 5 rows even. **Next Row:** K to marker, M1, k1, M1, k to end row. Rep last 6 rows once more—53 sts. Work even until hood measures approx 8" from beg, ending with a WS row and dec 1 st at center of last row—52 sts. Divide sts onto 2 needles and graft 26 sts from each side of hood tog as shown *below left*.

FINISHING
Set in sleeves. Join underarm and side seams. Sew zipper in place.

candy-cane cozies

photos on pages 36–37

SKILL LEVEL: Easy

MATERIALS:
Lion Brand Wool-Ease Sport-weight, Article 660, (435 yards per ball): One ball of Fisherman (099) for MC
Lion Brand, Wool-Ease, Article 620, worsted-weight yarn, (197 yards per ball): One ball of Cranberry (138) for CC

Size 4 (3.5 mm) knitting
needles or size needed to
obtain gauge
Tapestry needle

GAUGE:
In St st, 6 sts and 8 rows =
1"/2.5 cm. TAKE TIME TO
CHECK YOUR GAUGE.

SPECIAL ABBREVIATIONS:
Ssk: Slip next 2 sts knitwise
one at a time to right-hand
needle, insert tip of left
needle into fronts of these
two sts and k them together.

INSTRUCTIONS:
MITTEN (make two)
Finished Measurement =
2½ x 4"
With MC, cast on 30 sts.
*Leaving 8" tails when joining
colors, with MC, p 1 row, k 1
row, p 1 row. With CC, k 1
row. For Body Pattern, rep
from * for 6 total times. P 1
row with MC.
Top Shaping
Row 1: Maintaining stripe
pattern, (ssk, k11, k2tog) twice.
Row 2: P26.

Row 3: (Ssk, k9, k2tog) twice.
Row 4: P22.
Row 5: (K2tog) across.
Row 6: P11. Leaving a 12"
tail, cut yarn. Thread into
tapestry needle and back
through rem sts, twice.

FINISHING:
Take all tails to outside.
Matching stripes, tie each of
the 4 tails together in an
overhand knot all along side
edge. Trim to ½". With tail
from top, sew along side edge.
Let lower edge roll naturally.

CAP
Finished Measurement =
18 x 11"
Leaving a long tail, with MC,
cast on 120 sts. **Row 1 and
each following WS row:** P 1
row.
Row 2: K28, k2tog, ssk, k56,
k2tog, ssk, k28—116 sts.
Row 4: K27, k2tog, ssk, k54,
k2tog, ssk, k27—112 sts.

Rows 6-19: Cont in St st on
the 112 sts using MC.
Row 20: With MC, k11,
(k2tog, k20) 4 times,
k2tog, k11—107 sts.
*Note: When joining new color,
leave 8" tails at side edges.*
Row 21: P 1 row with MC.
Row 22: K with CC.
Row 23: P with MC.
Row 24: K with MC.
Row 25: P with MC.
Row 26: K with CC.
Row 27: P with MC.
Row 28: With MC, (k19,
k2tog) 5 times, k2.
Row 29: P102 with MC.
Rows 30–31: Rep Rows 22-23.
Row 32: With MC, (k18,
k2tog) 5 times, k2.
Row 33: With MC, p97.
Rows 34–35: Rep Rows 22-23.
Row 36: With MC, (k17,
k2tog) 5 times, k2.
Row 37: With MC, p92.
Continue in 4-row stripe
pattern, dec 5 sts evenly
spaced on each MC knit row
until 12 sts rem. Next Row:
K2tog across. P6. Cut yarn,
leaving an 8" tail. Thread
into tapestry needle and back
through sts. Draw up to
close opening. Sew to first
stripe row.

FINISHING:
Take all tails to outside.
Matching stripes, tie each of
the 4 tails together in an
overhand knot all along side
edge. With beginning tail at
lower edge, join MC rows up
to first stripe. Let this
portion form a natural roll.
Pom-Pom
Wind CC around a credit
card 25 times; carefully
remove card. Tie a separate
strand around center, tightly.
Cut ends. Trim and sew to
tip of cap.

cool school

CHAPTER 2

Kids will be super confident wearing and using these great-looking knits that earn an A+ in style. This lively chapter shares instructions for cardigans, vests, pullovers, hats, and backpacks that are just right for dashing off to class. To further expand your skills, crochet a pretty striped throw or a tote bag—two handy items to use while hitting the books.

gear

patterned

OFF-TO-CLASS
GUERNSEY PULLOVER
AND CAP

Rows of decorative stitches in pretty diamond and check patterns adorn this wool sweater and cap set. Knit in blueberry-color yarn, they're perfect to wear with jeans. Instructions begin on page 84.

SNAPPY RED VEST

When semicasual is the attire of the day, guys will love wearing this ribbed knit vest. The V-neck is just right to layer over a dress shirt. Instructions begin on page 86.

studious

DORM ROOM THROW

If you love to crochet or are eager to learn,
add this easy project to your must-do list.
Made with cotton/acrylic yarn, it's easy to wash.
Instructions begin on page 87.

hooked

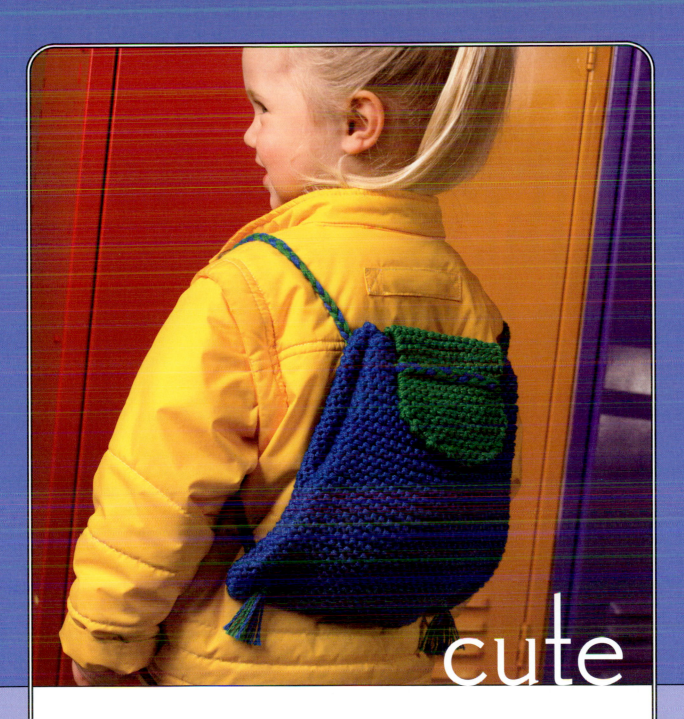

cute

READY-TO-GO BACKPACK

This handy backpack holds everything special to girls and boys. Knit in one piece with two strands of cotton yarn, the strapped bag has a flap to keep their treasures securely in place. Instructions begin on page 88.

CHIC CARDIGAN

Turn the easy-to-learn lace-box pattern into a button-up sweater that fends off the chill. This cardigan is pretty enough to wear with a skirt yet casual enough to wear with your favorite jeans. Instructions begin on page 89.

buttoned

simple

SASSY BOLERO

*Flaunt your retro style in a bolero vest knit
in mulberry and eggplant hues. After
knitting the graphic checks, add the garter-
stitch stripes at the edges for pizzazz.
Instructions begin on page 92.*

darling

SO-SWEET TANK

A playful palette of color dances on this soft cotton top. Sleeveless and hemmed with fluffy stitches, this tank will make your little one feel like a princess. Instructions begin on page 94.

CABLES-RIB VEST

Rich autumn colors are a handsome combination on this V-neck vest. The olive yarn carries to the edges with ribbing at the neck, armbands, and waist. Instructions begin on page 95.

boyish

artsy

GRANNY-SQUARE TOTE

Crocheted granny squares make a grand

comeback on this trendy tote.

Because the squares are worked individually,

this is a great take-along project.

Instructions begin on page 97.

WAFFLE-STITCH JACKET

Cropped, buttoned, and long-sleeved, this button-up cardigan is rich with style and texture. The loose fit works well for layering when there's a nip in the air. Instructions begin on page 98.

cuddly

BOOKWORM TUNIC

Soft cotton tape yarn in a cinnamon hue is used to create this long V-neck sweater blanketed with dotted checks. The neutral tone makes it a wardrobe staple. Instructions begin on page 101.

casual

off-to-class guernsey pullover and cap

photos on pages 66–67

SKILL LEVEL: Easy

SIZES: 4 (6, EIGHT, 10)
Note: The pattern is written for the smallest size with changes for larger sizes in parentheses. When only one number is given, it applies to all sizes. For ease in working, circle the numbers pertaining to the size you are knitting.

FINISHED MEASUREMENTS:
Chest: 28 (30, 33, 35)"
Length: 15½ (16½, 18, 20)"

MATERIALS:
Patons, Classic Merino Wool, 100% wool, worsted-weight yarn (223 yards per skein): For pullover and hat; 3 (4, 4, 5) skeins of Blueberry (213)
Size 7 (4.5 mm) knitting needles or size needed to obtain gauge
Size 6 (4.0 mm) knitting needles
2 stitch holders
Yarn needle

GAUGE:
In St st (knit RS rows, purl WS rows) with larger needles, 20 sts and 26 rows = 4"/10 cm. TAKE TIME TO CHECK YOUR GAUGE.

NOTE: *Read chart from right to left for RS rows and from left to right for WS rows.*

INSTRUCTIONS:
FRONT
** Beg at lower edge with smaller needles, cast on 67 (71, 79, 85) sts. Work Garter St (knit every row) for 7 (7, 9, 9) rows noting first row is WS and inc 4 sts evenly across last row—71 (75, 83, 89) sts. Change to larger needles and work in St st until work from beg measures approx 9½ (10, 11½, 13)", ending with a WS row. Work Chart Rows 1–23, noting 8 st rep will be worked 8 (9, 10, 11) times. **
Next Row (WS): Knit. Next 2 rows: Purl.
Neck Shaping
Next Row (RS): Work Row 4 of Chart across first 26 (27, 30, 33) sts (neck edge). Turn. Leave rem sts on a spare needle. Work 1 row even from chart. Keeping cont of chart, dec 1 st at neck edge on next and following alt rows 3 (4, 4, 5) times more—22 (22, 25, 27) sts. Cont working Chart until Row 15 of chart is complete. Cont in St st until work from beg measures approx 15½ (16½, 18, 20)", ending with a purl row.
Shoulder Shaping
Bind off 11 (11, 12, 13) sts beg next row. Work 1 row even. Bind off rem 11 (11, 13, 14) sts. With RS of work facing, slip center 19 (21, 23, 23) sts onto a st holder. Join yarn to rem sts and work to correspond to other side, reversing Chart pat and shaping.

BACK
Work from ** to ** as given for Front. Rep Rows 1 to 15 of Chart once more. Cont in St st until work from beg measures approx 15½ (16½, 18, 20)", ending with a purl row.
Shoulder Shaping
Bind off 11 (11, 12, 13) sts beg next 2 rows, then 11 (11, 13, 14) sts beg following 2 rows. Leave rem 27 (31, 33, 35) sts on a st holder.

SLEEVES (make two)

Beg at lower edge with smaller needles, cast on 35 (37, 37, 39) sts. Work Garter St for 7 (7, 9, 9) rows, noting first row is WS and inc 2 sts evenly across last row—37 (39, 39, 41) sts. Change to larger needles and work 6 rows in St st. Shape sides by inc 1 st each edge on next and every 6th (6th, 6th, 4th) row 8 (10, 12, 6) times, then on 6th rows 0 (0, 0, 10) times —55 (61, 65, 75) sts. Work even until sleeve measures approx 11 (13, 15, 16½)", ending with a purl row. Bind off.

FINISHING
Neckband

Sew right shoulder seam. With smaller needles, pick up and knit 11 (13, 13, 15) sts down left front neck edge. K19 (21, 23, 23) from Front st holder, dec 2 sts evenly across. Pick up and knit 11 (13, 13, 15) sts up right front neck edge. K27 (31, 33, 35) from Back st holder dec 3 sts evenly across—63 (73, 77, 83)

sts. Work 6 rows in Garter St. Bind off knitwise (WS). Sew left shoulder and neckband seam. Place markers on side edges of Front and Back 5½ (6, 6½, 7½)" down from shoulder seams. Set in sleeves between markers. Sew side and sleeve seams.

HAT

With smaller needles, cast on 81 (89, 89, 97) sts. Work 7 Garter St rows noting first row is WS. Change to larger needles and work 2 rows St st. Work Rows 17 to 23 of Chart as for size 10 of pullover noting 8 st rep will be worked 10 (11, 11, 12) times. Next Row (WS): Knit. Next 2 Rows: Purl. Work Rows 4 to 12 of chart as for size 10 of pullover, noting 8 st rep will be worked 10 (11, 11, 12) times. Next 2 Rows: Purl. Next Row: Knit. Beg with a knit row, work 2 rows St st, dec 2 (4, 4, 0) sts evenly across last row—79 (85, 85, 97) sts. **Top Shaping (RS):** K1; * k2tog, k11 (12, 12, 14). Rep from * 5 times more—73 (79, 79, 91) sts.

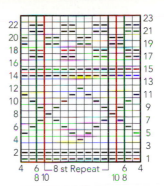

KEY

▬	Purl on RS, knit on WS
□	Knit on RS, purl on WS

Next Row: Purl. Next Row: K1; * k2tog, k10 (11, 11, 13). Rep from * 5 times more—67 (73, 73, 85) sts. Next Row: Purl. Cont in this manner, dec 6 sts evenly across next and following alt rows until there are 7 sts. Break yarn leaving a long end. Draw end through rem sts and fasten securely. Sew center back seam.

Make Tassel: Wind yarn around a piece of cardboard 4" wide approx 25 times. Remove cardboard and wrap yarn around loops ¾" below top edge. Tie yarn tightly through top loops. Cut through bottom loops. Sew tassel to top of Hat.

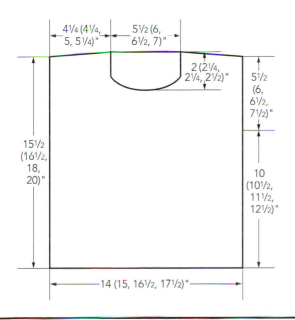

85

snappy red vest

photos on pages 68–69

SKILL LEVEL: Easy

SIZES: S (M, L, EXTRA-LARGE, XXL)
Note: The pattern is written for the smallest size with changes for larger sizes in parentheses. When only one number is given, it applies to all sizes. For ease in working, before you begin, circle the numbers pertaining to the size you are knitting.

FINISHED MEASUREMENTS:
Chest: 40 (42½, 45, 47½, 50)"
Length: 26 (26½, 27, 27½, 28)"

MATERIALS:
Brown Sheep, Top Of The Lamb, 100% wool, worsted-weight yarn (190 yards per skein): 6 (6, 7, 7, 8) skeins of Russet (200)
Size 8 (5 mm) knitting needles or size needed to obtain gauge

Size 6 (4 mm) knitting needles
Size 6 (4 mm) circular knitting needle, 24" long
One stitch holder
Yarn needle

GAUGE:
In Body Pattern with larger needles, 19 sts = 4"/10 cm; 40 rows = 6"/15 cm.
TAKE TIME TO CHECK YOUR GAUGE.

SPECIAL ABBREVIATIONS:
Ssk: Slip next 2 sts knitwise, one at a time to right-hand needle, insert tip of left-hand needle into front of these 2 sts and k them tog.

STITCHES USED:
Ribbing (a multiple of 2 sts + 1 st; a rep of 2 rows)
Row 1 (WS): P1; (k1, p1) across.
Row 2: K1; (p1, k1) across.
Rep Rows 1–2 for Ribbing.

Body Pattern (a multiple of 6 sts + 5 sts; a rep of 12 rows)
Row 1 (RS): Knit.
Row 2: Knit.
Row 3: Knit.
Row 4: Knit.
Row 5: K5; (p1, k5) across.
Row 6: P5; (k1, p5) across.
Rows 7–12: Rep Rows 5–6.
Rep Rows 1–12 for Body Pattern.

INSTRUCTIONS
BACK
Beg at the lower edge with smaller needles, cast on 95 (101, 107, 113, 119) sts. Work Ribbing to approx 3" from beg, ending with a WS row. Change to larger needles and Body Pattern. Work to approx 16½" from beg, ending with a WS row.
Armhole Shaping
Cont in pattern, bind off 6 sts at beg of next 2 rows. **Dec Row 1:** K1, ssk, work across to last 3 sts, k2tog, k1. Dec 1 st each edge every other row 5 (7, 8, 9, 11) times more. Work even on rem 71 (73, 77, 81, 83) sts to approx 26 (26½, 27, 27½, 28)" from beg, ending with a WS row.

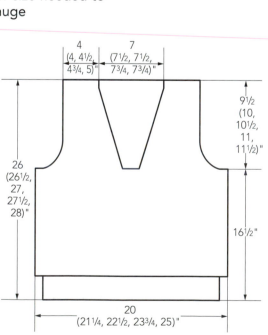

4
(4, 4½,
4¾, 5)"

7
(7½, 7½,
7¾, 7¾)"

9½
(10,
10½,
11,
11½)"

26
(26½,
27,
27½,
28)"

16½"

20
(21¼, 22½, 23¾, 25)"

86

Shoulder and Neck Shaping
Bind off 19 (19, 21, 22, 23) sts beg next 2 rows. Place rem 33 (35, 35, 37, 37) sts onto holder.

FRONT

Work as for Back until piece measures approx 16 (16½, 16½, 16½, 17)" from beg, end with a WS row. Place markers each side of center 7 sts.

V-Neck Shaping

Next Row: Working armhole shaping as for Back, pattern to marker, join a new ball of yarn and bind off center 7 sts, complete row. Working sides separately and at the same time, pattern across next WS row. **Dec Row 1:** Cont armhole decreases if necessary, pattern across to last 3 sts, k2tog, k1; for second side, k1, ssk, cont pattern across. Dec 1 st each neck edge every other row 3 (5, 5, 5, 5) times more and every sixth row 9 (8, 8, 9, 9) times. Cont as est on rem 19 (19, 21, 22, 23) sts for each shoulder until piece measures approx 26 (26½, 27, 27½, 28)" from beg, ending with a WS row. Bind off rem sts for each shoulder.

FINISHING

Join shoulder seams.
Neckband
With RS facing using circular needle, beg at right front neck edge, pick up and k52 (52, 52, 54, 54) sts evenly spaced to shoulder, k33 (35, 35, 37, 37) sts from holder, pick up and k52 (52, 52, 54, 54) sts evenly spaced along left neck edge. Work Ribbing on the

137 (139, 139, 145, 145) sts for approx 1½", ending with a WS row. Bind off in ribbing. Lapping left over right neckband, sew to lower edge of neck opening.
Armband (make two)
With RS facing using circular needle, pick up and k95 (99, 105, 109, 115) sts evenly spaced around armhole edge. Work 3 ribbing rows. Bind off in ribbing. Join side seams.

dorm room throw

photo on page 70

SKILL LEVEL: Easy

SIZE:
Approximately 30 × 42½", excluding fringe.

MATERIALS:
Lion Brand Yarn, Cotton-Ease, 50% cotton/50% acrylic yarn (207 yards per skein): 2 skeins each of Ice Blue (106) for A, Sugarplum (144) for B, Mint (156) for C, and Vanilla (100) for D.

Size 6/G (4 mm) aluminum crochet hook or size needed to obtain gauge

GAUGE
In Body Pattern, 15 sts and 10 rows = 4"/10 cm.
TAKE TIME TO CHECK YOUR GAUGE.

NOTES: Leave tails measuring approx 5" when beginning and ending rows. These tails will be incorporated into the fringe. This project is worked from side to side.

INSTRUCTIONS
Beginning at the side edge with A, ch 161. Sc in 2nd ch from hook and in each ch across—160 sts; turn.
Row 2: Ch 1, sc in each sc across. Fasten off.
Body Pattern
Row 1: With the RS facing, join B with a sl st in first sc. Ch 3 (counts as dc); * (skip next st, dc in next st, dc in skipped st—cross stitch made); rep from * across, ending dc in last st; turn.
Row 2: Ch 3 (counts as dc), dc in next dc; * cross stitch across to last 2 sts, dc in dc, dc in turning ch. Fasten off.

Row 3: With the RS facing, join C with a sl st in first dc. Rep Row 1.

Row 4: With C, rep Row 2.

Row 5: With the RS facing, join D with a sl st in first dc. Ch 1, sc in same dc as joining and in each dc across; turn.

Row 6: Ch 1, sc in each sc across; turn.

Rows 7–24: Rep Rows 1-6 three times in the following color sequence: (A, B, C); (D, A, B); (C, D, A).

Rep Rows 1–24 twice more.

FINISHING

Cut 5 strands of A measuring 9" each. Hold strands in a bundle; fold in half to form a loop. With the WS of throw facing, take loop through edge of first color A stripe. Take ends through loop and pull up to form a knot. Before tightening the knot, include any color A strands into the bundle. Adding one fringe to each sc stripe and 2 to each dc stripe, in color sequence add fringe across. Add fringe to the opposite edge. Trim fringe evenly.

ready-to-go backpack

photo on page 71

SKILL LEVEL: Easy

SIZE: 9 × 9"

MATERIALS:

Elmore Pisgah, Cotton Jewel, 100% cotton, worsted-weight yarn (77 yards per ball):

5 balls Capri Blue (32) for MC and 2 balls Leaf Green (52) for CC

Size 9 (5.5 mm) knitting needles or size needed to obtain gauge

One stitch marker

Yarn needle; safety pin

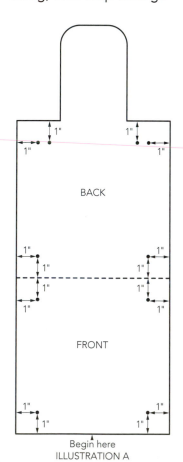

ILLUSTRATION A

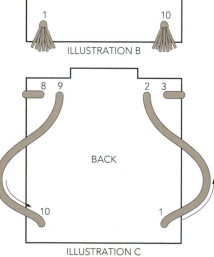

ILLUSTRATION B

ILLUSTRATION C

ILLUSTRATION D

GAUGE:
With 2 strands of yarn, in Garter Stitch (knit every row) 16 sts and 14 ridges = 4"/10 cm.
TAKE TIME TO CHECK YOUR GAUGE.

NOTE: The backpack is knitted in one piece and with a double strand of yarn.

INSTRUCTIONS:
Using 2 strands of MC, cast on 36 sts. Work Garter St to approx 18" from beg.
Flap: Bind off 10 sts, with 1 st on needle k next 15 sts, bind off rem 10 sts; turn.
Next Row (place marker in center of work to identify RS): Join CC and k across.
Cont k rows on 16 sts for 4", ending RS.
Next Row: K2tog, k to last 2 sts, k2tog.
* Next Row: K across.
Next Row: K2tog, k to last 2 sts, k2tog. **
Rep from * to ** again—10 sts.
Next Row: K2tog, bind off to last 2 sts, k2tog and fasten off.

FINISHING
With RS tog fold backpack in half lengthways and sew side seams, beg at top of backpack. Weave loose ends into WS of work. Turn RS out.

Shoulder Strap
Cut 6 blue and 6 green— 72" lengths of yarn. With 12 lengths of yarn tog, make double knot at one end, 1½" from end. Divide into 3 groups of 4 and braid to other end. Thread unknotted end through safety pin and thread through sts of

backpack—beg at #1 on Back Illustration C. Adjust length of shoulder loops and make double knot at other end of strap; trim ends.

chic cardigan

photos on pages 72–73

SKILL LEVEL: Intermediate

SIZES: XS (S, MEDIUM, L, XL)
Note: The pattern is written for the smallest size with changes for larger sizes in parentheses. When only one number is given, it applies to all sizes. For ease in working, before you begin, circle the numbers pertaining to the size you are knitting.

FINISHED MEASUREMENTS:
Bust (buttoned): 39 (42, 43, 46, 50)"
Length: 24½ (25, 25, 25½, 25½)"

MATERIALS:
Patons, Divine, 79.5% acrylic/ 18% mohair/2.5% polyester, bulky-weight yarn (142 yards per skein): 4 (5, 5, 5, 6) skeins of Soft Earth (06011)
Size 10 (6 mm) knitting needles or size needed to obtain gauge
Size 9 (5.5 mm) knitting needles
Three stitch holders
Seven 1-inch-diameter buttons
Yarn needle

GAUGE:
In Lace Box Pat with larger needles, 12 sts and 16 rows = 4"/10 cm. TAKE TIME TO CHECK YOUR GAUGE.

SPECIAL ABBREVIATIONS:
Sl1-k: Slip next stitch knitwise and with yarn on WS of fabric.
Sl1-k, k2tog, psso: Slip next stitch knitwise, k2tog, pass slipped stitch over k2tog.

Ssk: Slip next 2 sts knitwise, one at a time to right-hand needle, insert tip of left-hand needle into fronts of these 2 sts and k them tog.

INSTRUCTIONS:
BACK
Beg at lower edge with smaller needles, cast on 57 (60, 63, 66, 72) sts.
Row 1 (RS): K3 (0, 3, 0, 0); * p3, k3; rep from * to end of row.
Row 2: * P3, k3; rep from * to last 3 (0, 3, 0, 0) sts; p3 (0, 3, 0, 0).
Rep last 2 rows until work measures approx 3" from beg, ending with Row 2.

Change to larger needles and proceed as follows:
Row 1 (RS): P3 (0, 3, 0, 0); * k3, yo, sl1-k, k2tog, psso, yo; rep from * to last 6 sts; k3, p3.

Row 2: * K3, p3; rep from * to last 3 (0, 3, 0, 0) sts; k3 (0, 3, 0, 0).
Row 3: P3 (0, 3, 0, 0); * k3, p3; rep from * to end of row.
Row 4: Rep Row 2.
Row 5: P0 (3, 0, 3, 3); * k3, yo, sl1-k, k2tog, psso, yo; rep from * to last 3 sts; k3.
Row 6: P3; * k3, p3; rep from * to end of row, ending k0 (3, 0, 3, 3).
Row 7: P0 (3, 0, 3, 3); * k3, p3; rep from * to last 3 sts; k3.
Row 8: Rep Row 6.
These 8 rows form Lace Box Pat. Cont in Lace Box Pat until Back measures approx 16½" from beg, ending with a WS row.
Armhole Shaping
At the beg of the next 2 rows, bind off 4 (5, 5, 6, 7) sts —49 (50, 53, 54, 58) sts. Dec 1 st each end of needle on NEXT and following alt rows until there are 41 (42,

43, 44, 46) sts. Cont even in pat until armhole measures approx 8 (8½, 8½, 9, 9)", ending with a WS row.
Shoulder Shaping
Bind off 10 (10, 10, 10, 11) sts beg next 2 rows. Place rem 21 (22, 23, 24, 24) sts on a st holder.

LEFT FRONT
Beg at lower edge with smaller needles, cast on 27 (30, 30, 33, 36) sts.
Row 1 (RS): K3 (0, 0, 3, 0); * p3, k3; rep from * to end of row.
Row 2: * P3, k3; rep from * to last 3 (0, 0, 3, 0) sts; p3 (0, 0, 3, 0). Rep last 2 rows until work measures approx 3" from beg, ending with Row 2.

Change to larger needles and proceed as follows:
Row 1 (RS): P3 (0, 0, 3, 0); *k3, yo, sl1-k, k2tog, psso, yo; rep from * to last 6 sts; k3, p3.

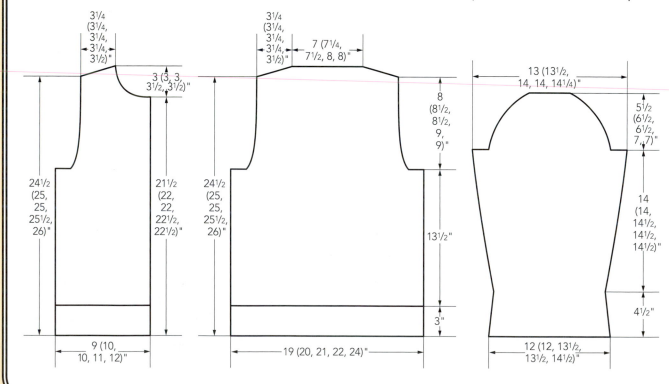

Row 2: * K3, p3; rep from * to last 3 (0, 0, 3, 0) sts; k3 (0, 0, 3, 0).
Row 3: P3 (0, 0, 3, 0); * k3, p3; rep from * to end of row.
Row 4: Rep Row 2.
Row 5: P0 (3, 3, 0, 3); * k3, yo, sl1-k, k2tog, psso, yo; rep from * to last 3 sts; k3.
Row 6: P3; * k3, p3; rep from * to last 0 (3, 3, 0, 3) sts; k0 (3, 3, 0, 3).
Row 7: P0 (3, 3, 0, 3); * k3, p3; rep from * to last 3 sts; k3.
Row 8: Rep Row 6.
These 8 rows form Lace Box Pat.
Cont in Lace Box Pat until Left Front measures approx 16.5" from beg, ending with a WS row.

Armhole and Front Shaping
Bind off 4 (5, 5, 6, 7) sts at beg of next row—23 (25, 25, 27, 29) sts.
Work 1 row even in pat.
Dec 1 st at beg of NEXT and following alt rows until there are 19 (21, 20, 22, 23) sts.
Cont even in pat until armhole measures approx 5 (5½, 5½, 5½, 5½)", ending with a WS row.

Neck Shaping
Next Row: Pat to last 5 (6, 6, 6, 6) sts (neck edge); slip last 5 (6, 6, 6, 6) sts onto a st holder.
Work 1 row even in pat.

Sizes S, L and XL only: Dec 1 st at neck edge on next 3 rows. Work 1 row even in pat.

All Sizes: Dec 1 st at neck edge on next and following alt rows until there are 10 (10, 10, 10, 11) sts. Cont even in pat until armhole measures approx 8 (8½, 8½, 9, 9)", ending with a WS row. Bind off.

RIGHT FRONT
Beg at lower edge with smaller needles, cast on 27 (30, 30, 33, 36) sts.
Row 1 (RS): * K3, p3; rep from * to last 3 (0, 0, 3, 0) sts; k3 (0, 0, 3, 0).
Row 2: P3 (0, 0, 3, 0); * k3, p3; rep from * to end of row.
Rep last 2 rows until work measures approx 3" from beg, ending with Row 2.

Change to larger needles and proceed as follows:
Row 1 (RS): P3; * k3, yo, sl1-k, k2tog, psso, yo; rep from * to last 6 (3, 3, 6, 3) sts; k3, p3 (0, 0, 3, 0).
Row 2: P0 (3, 3, 0, 3); * k3, p3; rep from * to last 3 sts; k3.
Row 3: * P3, k3; rep from * to last 3 (0, 0, 3, 0) sts; p3 (0, 0, 3, 0).
Row 4: Rep Row 2.
Row 5: * K3, yo, sl1-k, k2tog, psso, yo; rep from * to last 3 (6, 6, 3, 6) sts; k3, p0 (3, 3, 0, 3).
Row 6: K0 (3, 3, 0, 3); * p3, k3; rep from * to last 3 sts; p3.
Row 7: * K3, p3; rep from * to last 3 (0, 0, 3, 0) sts; k3 (0, 0, 3, 0).
Row 8: Rep Row 6.
These 8 rows form Lace Box Pat.
Cont in Lace Box Pat working Right Front to correspond to Left Front, reversing all shapings.

SLEEVES (make two)
Beg at lower edge with larger needles, cast on 36 (36, 40, 40, 44) sts.
Row 1 (RS): * K4, p4; rep from * to last 4 (4, 0, 0, 4) sts; k4 (4, 0, 0, 4).
Row 2: P4 (4, 0, 0, 4); * k4, p4; rep from * to end of row.

Rep last 2 rows until work measures approx 2.5" from beg, ending with Row 1.
Next Row (WS): (P1, p2tog, p1) 1 (1, 0, 0, 1) time; * k1, k2tog, k1, p1, p2tog, p1; rep from * to end of row—27 (27, 30, 30, 33) sts.

Change to smaller needles and cont in ribbing until work measures approx 4½" ending with a WS row.

Change to larger needles and proceed as follows:
Row 1 (RS): P3 (3, 0, 0, 3); * k3, yo, sl1-k, k2tog, psso, yo; rep from * to last 6 sts; k3, p3.
Row 2: * K3, p3; rep from * to last 3 (3, 0, 0, 3) sts; k3 (3, 0, 0, 3).
Lace Box Pat is now in position.
Cont in est pat shaping sides by inc 1 st each edge on NEXT and every 8th (6th, 8th, 8th, 10th) row 5 (2, 5, 5, 4) times—39 (33, 42, 42, 43) sts, taking inc sts into Lace Box St Pat.

Size S only: Inc 1 st each edge on following 8th rows 4 times—41 sts, taking inc sts into Lace Box St Pat.

All Sizes: Work even in pat to approx 18½ (18½, 19, 19, 19)", ending with a WS row.

Sleeve Cap Shaping
Keeping cont of est pat, bind off 2 (2, 2, 3, 3) sts beg next 2 rows—35 (37, 38, 36, 37) sts. Dec 1 st each end of needle on NEXT and following alt rows until there are 23 (23, 24, 16, 17) sts, then on every row until there are 5 (5, 6, 6, 7) sts. Bind off rem sts.

FINISHING

Button Band: With smaller needles, cast on 7 sts.
Row 1 (RS): K2, (p1, k1) twice, k1.
Row 2: (K1, p1) 3 times, k1. Rep last 2 rows until band, when slightly stretched, measures length to fit up left front edge to neck edge, sewing in place as you work. Do not bind off. Leave 7 sts on a safety pin. Place 7 button markers on this band having bottom button ½" above cast on edge, top button ½" below neck edge and rem 5 buttons spaced evenly between.

Buttonhole Band
Work as given for Button Band, sewing to right front and working buttonholes to correspond to markers as follows: **Row 1 (RS):** K2, p1, yo, ssk, k2.
Sew shoulder seams. Sew side and sleeve seams. Set in sleeves.

Collar
With RS facing and smaller needles, rib across 7 sts on Right Front safety pin as follows: K2, (p1, k1) twice, p1; k5 (6, 6, 6, 6) from Right Front st holder; pick up and knit 11 (11, 11, 13, 13) sts up Right Front neck edge; k21 (22, 23, 24, 24) from Back st holder, dec 0 (1, 0, 1, 1) st at center; pick up and knit 11 (11, 11, 13, 13) sts down Left Front neck edge; k5 (6, 6, 6, 6) from Left Front st holder; rib across 7 sts on Left Front safety pin as follows: (p1, k1) 3 times, k1—67 (69, 71, 75, 75) sts.
Cont in ribbing until Collar measures approx 8" from beg, ending with a WS row. Bind off in r.b.
Sew buttons in position.

sassy bolero

photos on pages 74–75

SKILL LEVEL: Intermediate

SIZES: S (MEDIUM, L, XL)

Note: The pattern is written for the smallest size with changes for larger sizes in parentheses. When only one number is given, it applies to all sizes. For ease in working, before you begin, circle the numbers pertaining to the size you are knitting.

FINISHED MEASUREMENTS:
Bust: 30 (35, 41, 47)"
Length: 14 (15½, 17, 17)"

MATERIALS:
Muench Yarns, Maxima, 100% merino wool, DK-weight yarn, (110 meters per ball): 2 (3, 3, 4) balls EACH of Mulberry (G152-018) for color A and Eggplant (G152-021) for color B
Size 7 (4.5 mm) knitting needles or size needed to obtain gauge
Size F/5 (3.75 mm) crochet hook
Safety pin for marker
Tapestry needle

GAUGE:
In Garter St (knit every row) and color pattern, 20 sts and 38 rows = 4"/10 cm.
TAKE TIME TO CHECK YOUR GAUGE.

SPECIAL ABBREVIATIONS:
Yf: Take yarn to front or RS of fabric.
Sssk: Slip next 3 sts knitwise, one at a time to right-hand needle, insert tip of left-hand needle into front of these 3 sts and k them together.
Ssk: Slip next 2 sts knitwise, one at a time to right-hand needle, insert tip of left-hand needle into fronts of these 2 sts and k them together.

Note: Use separate strands for each color section. The striped body band is added after the vest has been joined together.

INSTRUCTIONS:
BACK
Beg at lower edge, cast on (7 sts B, 7 sts A) for 5 (6, 7, 8) times, cast on 7 sts B—77 (91, 105, 119) sts.

Row 1 (WS): K7–B; * bring next color from under present color and k7–A, bring next color from under present color and k7–B; rep from * across.

Row 2: K7–B; * yf, take next color under last color and to WS, k7–A, yf, take next color under last color and to WS, k7–B; rep from * across.

Rows 3–12: Rep Rows 1-2.

Row 13: (K1–A, k1–B) across, ending k1–A.

Row 14 (RS): As Row 2, beg with k7–A and alternating color blocks across.

Row 15: As Row 1, in newly est color block pattern.

Rows 16–25: As Rows 14-15.

Row 26: As Row 14.

Row 27: (K1–B, k1–A) across, ending k1-B.

Row 28: As Row 2.

Row 29: As Row 1.

Rows 30–39: As Rows 28-29.

Row 40: As Row 28.

Rep Rows 13–40 for Body Pattern until piece measures approx 5¼" from beg, ending with a WS row.

Armhole Shaping
Bind off 5 sts at beg of next 2 rows. **Dec Row:** Keeping to est color and st pattern, k2, sssk, pattern across, ending k3tog, k2. Work 1 row even. Rep last 2 rows for 3 (4, 6, 7) times more—51 (61, 67, 77) sts. Work even to approx 12½ (14, 15½, 15½)" from beg, ending with a WS row.

Neck Shaping
Pattern across 12 (15, 17, 21) sts, join new balls of yarn and bind off center 27 (31, 33, 35) sts, pattern to end of row. Working sides separately and at the same time, dec 1 st each neck edge, twice. *NOTE:* On dec row, work to last 4 sts, k2tog, k2; for next side, k2, ssk, work to end. When piece measures approx 13 (14½, 16, 16)" from beg, end with a WS row. Bind off rem 10 (13, 15, 19) sts for each shoulder.

LEFT FRONT
Beg at lower edge, cast on (7 sts A, 7 sts B) for 1 (1, 2, 2) time(s), with A cast on 2 (7, 2, 7) sts, with B cast on 0 (2, 0, 2) sts—16 (23, 30, 37) total sts. In est color pattern, knit across. **Inc Row (RS):** Pattern across, ending inc 1 st in last st. Pattern is now set. Including new sts into color block pattern, inc 1 st at front edge every RS row 16 times more—33 (40, 47, 54) sts. Place a marker on last inc row. When piece measures approx 5¼" from beg cast on row, end with a WS row.

Armhole Shaping
Bind off 5 sts at beg of next row. **Dec Row (RS):** K2, sssk, pattern across. Rep Dec Row every RS row 3 (4, 6, 7) times more. AT SAME TIME, cont even until work from marker measures 3", end with a WS row.

Neck Shaping
Dec Row: Pattern across to last 4 sts, k2tog, k2. Next 3 Rows: Pattern across. Rep last 4 rows 3 (4, 8, 8) times more, then dec every other row 6 (7, 4, 5) times. Cont in pattern on rem 10 (13, 15, 19) sts to same length as Back.

RIGHT FRONT
Beg at lower edge, cast on 2 sts with A (B, A, B); * cast on 7 sts with B (A, B, A), cast on 7 sts with A (B, A, B). Rep from * 0 (0, 1, 1) time more, cast on 0 (7, 0, 7) sts with A— 16 (23, 30, 37) sts. In est color pattern, knit across. **Inc Row (RS):** Inc 1, pattern across. Work as for Left Front, rev front, armhole and neck shaping. For Armhole decrease; pattern to last 5 sts, k3tog, k2. For Neck Shaping: k2, ssk, pattern to end.

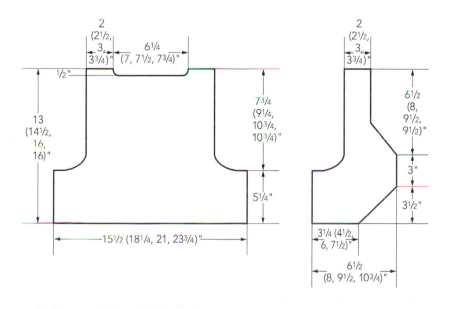

FINISHING
Join shoulder and side seams.
Armhole Edging (make two)
With RS facing, using crochet hook and color B, slip st evenly around armhole, beg and ending at underarm seam. In first slip st (slip st, ch 1, sc); (ch 1, skip 1 slip st, sc in next slip st) around, ending ch 1, skip 1 slip st, slip st in first sc. Fasten off.
Body Band
With color B, cast on 5 sts. (K2 rows B, k2 rows A) until band fits around entire edge of body. Beg at back neck, sew band in place and sew band edges tog. Weave in loose ends on WS of fabric.

so-sweet tank

photos on pages 76–77

SKILL LEVEL: Easy

SIZES: 4 (SIX, 8, 10)
Note: *The pattern is written for the smallest size with changes for larger sizes in parentheses. When only one number is given, it applies to all sizes. For ease in working, before you begin, circle the numbers pertaining to the size you are knitting.*

FINISHED MEASUREMENTS:
Chest: 25 (27, 29, 31)"
Length: 11½ (12½, 14, 15½)"

MATERIALS:
Berroco, Cotton Twist, 70% cotton/30% rayon, worsted-weight yarn (85 yards per skein): 3 (4, 4, 5) skeins of Secret Garden (8461) for MC
Berroco, Plume FX, 100% polyester, novelty weight yarn (63 yards per skein): 1 skein of Purple (6741) for A
Size 8 (5 mm) knitting needles or size needed to obtain gauge
Size 6 (4 mm) knitting needles
2 stitch holders
Yarn needle

GAUGE:
In St st (knit RS rows, purl WS rows) with larger needles and MC, 19 sts and 26 rows = 4"/10 cm.
TAKE TIME TO CHECK YOUR GAUGE.

SPECIAL ABBREVIATIONS:
MK: P3tog without taking sts off needle, k3tog, then p3tog same 3 sts. Slip sts off needle.
Ssk: Slip next 2 sts knitwise, one at a time to right-hand needle, insert tip of left-hand needle into fronts of these 2 sts and k them tog.

INSTRUCTIONS:
BACK
** Beg at lower edge with smaller needles and 1 strand each of MC and A, cast on 52 (56, 59, 62) sts. Work Garter St (knit every row) for 9 rows, noting first row is WS and inc 7 (9, 10, 11) sts evenly across last row—59 (65, 69, 73) sts. Break A. Change to larger needles and work in pat with MC only as follows:
Row 1 (RS): Knit.
Row 2 and alt rows: Purl.
Row 3: K4 (3, 1, 3); * MK, k5. Rep from * across, ending MK, k4 (3, 1, 3).
Rows 5 and 7: Knit.
Row 9: K8 (7, 5, 7); * MK, k5. Rep from * across, ending MK, k8 (7, 5, 7).
Row 11: Knit.
Row 12: Purl.
These 12 rows form pat.

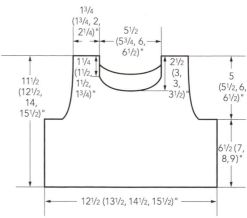

Cont in pat until work from beg measures approx 6½ (7, 8, 9)", ending with a WS row.

Armhole Shaping
Keeping cont of pat, bind off 3 (4, 5, 5) sts beg next 2 rows —53 (57, 59, 63) sts. **Next Row (RS):** K2, k2tog, pat across, ending ssk, k2. **Next Row:** Purl. Rep last 2 rows 3 (4, 4, 4) times more—45 (47, 49, 53) sts.** Cont even in pat until piece measures approx 10¼ (11, 12½, 13¾)" from beg, ending with a WS row.
Neck Shaping
Pat across 12 (12, 14, 15) sts (neck edge). Turn. Leave rem sts on a spare needle. Work 1 row even in pat. Dec 1 st at neck edge on NEXT and following alt rows 2 (2, 3, 3) times more—9 (9, 10, 11) sts. Cont in pat until piece measures approx 11½ (12½, 14, 15½)" from beg, ending with a WS row. Bind off. With RS of work facing, slip center 21 (23, 21, 23) sts onto a st holder. Join MC to rem sts and work to correspond to other side, reversing shaping.

FRONT
Work from ** to ** as given for Back. Cont even in pat until piece measures approx 9 (9½, 11, 12)" from beg, ending with a WS row.
Neck Shaping
Pat across 14 (14, 16, 17) sts (neck edge). Turn. Leave rem sts on a spare needle. Work 1 row even in pat. Dec 1 st at neck edge on NEXT and following alt rows 4 (4, 5, 5) times more—9 (9, 10, 11) sts. Cont in pat until piece measures approx 11½ (12½, 14, 15½)" from beg, ending with a WS row. Bind off.

With RS of work facing, slip center 17 (19, 17, 19) sts onto a st holder. Join MC to rem sts and work to correspond to other side, reversing shaping.

FINISHING
Neckband
Sew right shoulder seam. With smaller needles and MC, pick up and knit 13 (15, 15, 17) sts down left front neck edge. K17 (19, 17, 19) from front st holder, dec 2 (2, 0, 2) sts evenly across. Pick up and knit 13 (15, 15, 17) sts up right front neck edge and 7 (8, 8, 10) sts down right back neck edge. K21 (23, 21, 23) from back st holder dec 0 (3, 0, 3) sts evenly across. Pick up and knit 7 (8, 8, 10) sts up left back neck edge—76 (83, 84, 91) sts. Work 4 rows Garter St. Bind off knitwise (WS). Sew left shoulder and neckband seam.
Armbands: With smaller needles and MC, pick up and knit 56 (62, 66, 70) sts evenly along armhole edge. Work 4 rows Garter St. Bind off knitwise (WS). Sew side and armband seams.

cables-rib vest
photo on page 78

SKILL LEVEL: Intermediate

SIZES: 6 (EIGHT, 10, 12, 14)
Note: The pattern is written for the smallest size with changes for larger sizes in parentheses. When only one number is given, it applies to all sizes. For ease in working, before you begin, circle the numbers pertaining to the size you are knitting.

FINISHED MEASUREMENTS:
Chest: 31 (32½, 34½, 36, 37½)"
Length: 17½ (17½, 18, 18½, 19)"

95

MATERIALS:
Patons, Classic Merino Wool, 100% wool, worsted-weight yarn (223 yards per skein): 1 (1, 2, 2, 2) skeins of Deep Olive (205) for MC; 1 skein each of Russet (206) for A, Chestnut (231) for B, Paprika (238) for C, Rich Red (207) for D, and Natural Mix (229) for E

Size 7 (4.5 mm) knitting needles or size needed to obtain gauge

Size 6 (4 mm) knitting needles

Size 6 (4 mm) circular needle, 24" long

Stitch holder

Cable needle (cn)

Yarn needle

GAUGE:
In St st (knit RS rows, purl WS rows) with larger needles, 20 sts and 26 rows = 4"/10 cm. TAKE TIME TO CHECK YOUR GAUGE.

SPECIAL ABBREVIATIONS:
Cr6B (over 6 sts): Slip next 4 sts onto cn and leave at back of work. K2, then bring yarn to front of work. Slip 2 purl sts from cn back onto left-hand needle and purl them. Slip rem 2 sts from cn onto left-hand needle and knit them

Ssk: Slip next 2 sts knitwise, one at a time to right-hand needle, insert tip of left-hand needle into fronts of these 2 sts and k them tog.

INSTRUCTIONS:
BACK
** Beg at lower edge with MC and smaller needles cast on 82 (82, 86, 86, 94) sts.
Ribbing, Row 1 (RS): P0 (0, 2, 2, 0); * k2, p2; rep from * across, ending k2 (2, 0, 0, 2).
Row 2: K0 (0, 2, 2, 0); * p2, k2; rep from * to across, ending p2 (2, 0, 0, 2). Rep Ribbing Rows 1–2 until work measures approx 3½ (3½, 3½, 4, 4)" from beg, ending with Row 2.
Cable Row: P0 (0, 2, 2, 0), (k2, p2) twice; * Cr6B, p2, k2, p2; rep from * across, ending k2, p0 (0, 2, 2, 0). Work 7 more rows of Ribbing and adjust stitch number by dec 4 (dec 0, dec 0, inc 4, inc 0) sts evenly across last row—78 (82, 86, 90, 94) sts.

Change to larger needles and proceed in St st Stripe pat as follows:
Rows 1–4: A.
Rows 5–8: B.
Rows 9–12: C.
Rows 13–16: D.
Rows 17–20: E.
Rows 21–24: MC.
These 24 rows form Stripe Pat. Cont in Stripe Pat until work from beg measures approx 10½ (10½, 10½, 11, 11)" ending with a WS row.

Armhole Shaping
Keeping cont of Stripe Pat, bind off 5 (6, 6, 6, 7) sts beg next 2 rows—68 (70, 74, 78, 80) sts. ** Next Row: K2, k2tog, pat to last 4 sts, ssk, k2. Work 1 row even. Rep last 2 rows 4 (4, 5, 6, 6) times more—58 (60, 62, 64, 66) sts. Cont even in pat until piece measures approx 17½ (17½, 18, 18½, 19)" from beg, ending with a WS row.

Shoulder Shaping
Bind off 7 (7, 7, 8, 8) sts beg next 2 rows, then 7 (8, 8, 8, 8) sts beg following 2 rows. Leave rem 30 (30, 32, 32, 34) sts on a st holder.

FRONT
Work from ** to ** as for Back.
Neck Shaping
Left Shoulder: K2, k2tog, pat across 26 (27, 29, 31, 32) sts, ssk, k2 (neck edge); turn, leave rem sts on a spare needle. Work 1 row even.
Next Row: K2, k2tog, pat to last 4 sts, ssk, k2. Rep last 2 rows 3 (3, 4, 5, 5) times more —24 (25, 25, 25, 26) sts. Dec 1 st at neck edge only on

2³⁄₄ (3, 3, 3¼, 3¼)"

6 (6, 6¼, 6¼, 6¾)"

17½ (17½, 18, 18½, 19)"

7 (7, 7½, 7½, 8)"

5½"

5 (5, 5, 5½, 5½)"

15½ (16¼, 17¼, 18, 18¾)"

following alt rows until there are 18 (19, 19, 21, 22) sts, then on every 4th row until there are 14 (15, 15, 16, 16) sts. Cont even in pat until piece measures approx 17½ (17½, 18, 18½, 19)" from beg, ending with a WS row.

Shoulder Shaping
Bind off 7 (7, 7, 8, 8) sts beg next row. Purl 1 row. Bind off rem 7 (8, 8, 8, 8) sts.

Right Shoulder: With RS of work facing, join yarn to rem sts and work to correspond to first side, reversing all shapings.

FINISHING
Sew shoulder seams.
Neckband: With RS of work facing, MC and circular needle, pick up and knit 39 (39, 42, 42, 43) sts up right front neck edge. K30 (30, 32, 32, 34) from back st holder. Pick up and knit 39 (39, 42, 42, 43) sts down left front neck edge—108 (108, 116, 116, 120) sts. Do not join. Working back and forth across needle in rows, proceed:

Row 1 (WS): P3; * k2, p2; rep from * to last 5 sts, k2, p3.
Row 2: K3; * p2, k2; rep from * to last 5 sts, p2, k3. Rep last 2 rows once more, then Row 1 once. Bind off in ribbing. Place right front over left front and sew sides of neckband in position.
Armbands: With RS of work facing, MC and smaller needles, pick up and knit 86 (86, 90, 90, 94) sts along armhole edge. **Row 1 (WS):** * P2, k2; rep from * to last 2 sts, p2. **Row 2:** * K2, p2, rep from * to last 2 sts, k2. Rep last 2 rows once more, then Row 1 once. Bind off in ribbing. Sew side and armband seams.

granny-square tote

photo on page 79

SKILL LEVEL: Easy

SIZE: Approx 12½" tall and 16" wide.

MATERIALS:
Lion Brand, Wool-Ease Chunky, 80% acrylic/20% wool, chunky-weight yarn (153 yards per ball): 2 balls of Charcoal (152) for A; 1 ball each of Walnut (127) for B, Appleton (141) for C, and Foliage (187) for D
Size J/10 (6 mm) crochet hook or size needed to obtain gauge
Yarn needle

GAUGE:
Rnds 1–2 of Granny Square— 3.5"/9cm square.
In sc, 11 sts and 12 rows— 4"/10 cm.
TAKE TIME TO CHECK YOUR GAUGE.

INSTRUCTIONS:
First Granny Square
Rnd 1: With A, ch 4; join with sl st to form a ring. Ch 3 (counts as dc), 2 dc in ring; (ch 3, 3 dc in ring) 3 times, ch 3; join with sl st in third ch of beg ch-3. Fasten off.
Rnd 2: With RS facing, join B with sl st in any ch-3 sp. Ch 3 (counts as dc), in same ch-3 sp (2 dc, ch 3, 3 dc). * Ch 1, in next ch-3 sp (3 dc, ch 3, 3 dc); rep from * twice more, ch 1, join with sl st in third ch of beg ch-3. Fasten off.

First Side, First Row
(from left to right)
Second Granny—D for Rnd 1 and C for Rnd 2.
Third Granny—B for 1 and D for 2.
Fourth Granny—C for 1 and B for 2.
Fifth (side) Granny—B for 1 and D for 2.
First Side, Second Row
(from left to right)
First Granny—C for 1 and D for 2.
Second Granny—C for 1 and A for 2.
Third Granny—B for 1 and C for 2.
Fourth Granny—A for 1 and D for 1.
Fifth (side) Granny—D for 1 and C for 2.
Using A, sew squares tog through back loops in order given. Join Second Row to First Row.
Second Side
As for First Side. Join rem side edge to form top of tote.

LOWER SIDES
With RS facing and A, work 11 sc along edge of each Granny on Front—44 sts; turn. **Row 2:** Ch 1, sc in each sc across; turn. Rep Row 2 for a total of 25 rows. Fasten off. Rep as est for Back. For each side, work 11 sc along edge of Granny and then work 24 more sc rows. Fold front in half so that 13 rows are on front and 12 rows are on back of fabric. **To Join:** With A, slip st along side, in corner (sl st, ch 1, sl st), sl st along bottom, work corner and then work along side. Rep this process for each of the rem 3 sections. (The inside folds form pockets).

Thread A into yarn needle and join sections by sewing through the slip sts.

BASE
Holding B and C tog, ch 12. Sc in second ch from hook and in each ch across—11 sts; turn. **Row 2:** Ch 1, sc in each sc across; turn. Rep Row 2 for a total of 37 rows. Fasten off. Using A, sew Base to Lower Sides through the slip sts.
Top Edging
Beg at one side, join A. Ch 1, sc in same sp and in each st around, working sc2tog (draw up a lp in each of next 2 sts, yo and draw through all 3 lps on hook) over each joining. Next Row: Ch 1, working left to right for Reverse Sc, (sc in 3 sc, sk 1 sc) around. At end, fasten off.

HANDLE (make two)
Cut 13 strands of B measuring 18" long. Hold strands in a bundle and tie an overhand knot near each end. With B, make a slip knot on hook then sc around the bundle over and over until it is firmly covered between knots. Ch 1, work Reverse Sc across as follows: (sk 1 sc, sc in next sc). At end, fasten off. Hide ends. Take handle knots from front to back and through ch-1 space of Granny Rnd 2 on Squares 2 and 3 of Front and Back. With B, sew securely in place.

FINISHING
Hide ends. Fold side edges in half and toward inside of tote. With A, tack in place.

waffle-stitch jacket

photos on pages 80–81

SKILL LEVEL: Intermediate

SIZES: XS (S, MEDIUM, L, XL)

Note: The pattern is written for the smallest size with changes for larger sizes in parentheses. When only one number is given, it applies to all sizes. For ease in working, before you begin, circle the numbers pertaining to the size you are knitting.

FINISHED MEASUREMENTS:
Bust (buttoned): 35 (38½, 40½, 41½, 44)"
Length: 22 (22½, 22½, 23, 23½)"

MATERIALS:
Patons, UpCountry, 100% wool, bulky-weight yarn (78 yards per skein): 6 (6, 7, 7, 8) skeins of Oak (80914) for MC and 4 (4, 4, 5, 5) skeins of Soft Cream (80906) for A
Size 10.5 (6.5 mm) knitting needles or size needed to obtain gauge
Size 10 (6 mm) knitting needles
Size J/10 (6 mm) crochet hook
Three buttons; yarn needle

GAUGE:
In Waffle Stitch Pattern with larger needles, 9½ sts and 20 rows = 4"/10 cm.
TAKE TIME TO CHECK YOUR GAUGE.

SPECIAL ABBREVIATIONS:
K1-B: Knit into next st, one row below, at same time, slip off st above.

STITCHES USED:
Waffle St (a multiple of 2 sts + 1 st; a rep of 4 rows)
Row 1 (WS): With MC, knit.
Row 2: With MC; * k1, k1-B; rep from * to last st, k1.
Row 3: With A, knit.
Row 4: With A, k2; * k1-B, k1; rep from * to last 3 sts; k1-B, k2.
Rep Rows 1–4 for Waffle St Pat.

NOTE: *Crochet trim on all outside edges is not reflected on the diagrams.*

INSTRUCTIONS:
BACK
Beg at lower edge with larger needles and MC, cast on 41 (45, 47, 49, 51) sts. Work Waffle St Pat for 7 rows.
Side Shaping
Keeping cont of pat, dec 1 st each end of needle on NEXT

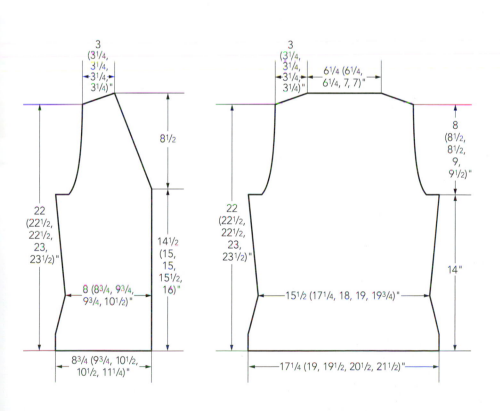

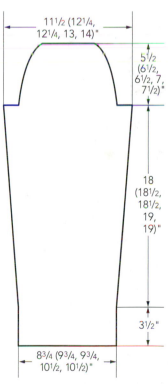

and following 10th row—37 (41, 43, 45, 47) sts. Cont even in pat until Back measures approx 6" from beg, ending with a WS row. Work 4 rows even in pat. Inc 1 st each end of needle on NEXT and following 16th row —41 (45, 47, 49, 51) sts. Cont even in pat until Back measures approx 14", ending with a WS row.

Armhole Shaping
At the beg of the next 2 rows, bind off 3 (3, 4, 4, 5) sts —35 (39, 39, 41, 41) sts. Dec 1 st each end of needle on NEXT and following alt rows until there are 29 (31, 31, 33, 33) sts. Cont even in pat until armhole measures approx 8 (8½, 8½, 9, 9½)", ending with a WS row.

Shoulder Shaping
Bind off 3 (4, 4, 4, 4) sts beg next 2 rows, then 4 sts beg following 2 rows. Bind off rem 15 (15, 15, 17, 17) sts.

LEFT FRONT
Beg at lower edge with larger needles and MC, cast on 21 (23, 25, 25, 27) sts. Work Waffle St Pat for 7 rows.

Side Shaping
Keeping cont of pat, dec 1 st at beg of NEXT and following 10th row—19 (21, 23, 23, 25) sts. Cont even in pat until Left Front measures approx 6" from beg, ending with a WS row. Work 4 rows even in pat. Inc 1 st at beg of next and following 16th row—21 (23, 25, 25, 27) sts. Cont even in pat until Left Front measures approx 14", ending with a WS row.

Armhole and Front Shaping
Bind off 3 (3, 4, 4, 5) sts at beg of next row—18 (20, 21, 21, 22) sts. Work 1 row even in pat. At armhole edge, dec 1 st every other row 0 (2, 1, 2, 3) time(s)—18 (18, 20, 19, 19) sts. Work 1 row even. Dec 1 st at front edge on NEXT row, then on following 4th rows 7 (7, 8, 8, 9) times more. AT SAME TIME, dec 1 st at armhole edge every other row 3 (2, 3, 2, 1) time(s) —7 (8, 8, 8, 8) sts. Cont even in pat until armhole measures approx 8 (8½, 8½, 9, 9½)", ending with a WS row.

Shoulder Shaping
Bind off 3 (4, 4, 4, 4) sts beg next row. Work 1 row even in pat. Bind off rem 4 sts.

RIGHT FRONT
Beg at lower edge with larger needles and MC, cast on 21 (23, 25, 25, 27) sts. Work Waffle St Pat for 7 rows.

Side Shaping
Keeping cont of pat, dec 1 st at end of NEXT and following 10th row—19 (21, 23, 23, 25) sts. Cont even in pat until Left Front measures approx 6" from beg, ending with a WS row. Work 4 rows even in pat. Inc 1 st at end of next and following 16th row—21 (23, 25, 25, 27) sts. Cont even in pat until Left Front measures approx 14", ending with a RS row.

Armhole and Front Shaping
Bind off 3 (3, 4, 4, 5) sts at beg of next row—18 (20, 21, 21, 22) sts. Reversing shaping, work as for Left Front.

SLEEVES (make two)
Beg at lower edge with smaller needles, cast on 26 (28, 28, 30, 30) sts. Work 3½" in Garter St (knit every row noting first row is RS of Cuff), dec 5 sts evenly across last row—21 (23, 23, 25, 25) sts. Place markers at each end of last row. Change to larger needles and work Waffle St Pat (noting first row is WS) for 7 rows. Cont in est pat shaping sides by inc 1 st each edge on NEXT and every 14th row 2 (2, 2, 2, 3) times— 27 (29, 29, 31, 33) sts, taking inc sts into Waffle St Pat. Work even in pat to approx 18 (18½, 18½, 19, 19)" from markers, ending with a WS row.

Cap Shaping
Keeping cont of est pat, bind off 3 (3, 4, 4, 5) sts beg next 2 rows—21 (23, 21, 23, 23) sts. Dec 1 st each end of needle on NEXT and following 4th row 3 (5, 6, 7, 6) times more, every 6th row 0 (0, 0, 0, 1) time and every 2nd row 4 (3, 1, 0, 0) times. Work 1 row even in pat. Bind off rem 5 (5, 5, 7, 7) sts.

FINISHING
COLLAR: With smaller needles and MC, cast on 5 sts.
Row 1 (WS): Knit.
Row 2: Knit to last 2 sts, inc 1 st in next st, k1 (outer edge). Rep last 2 rows until there are 11 sts, then inc 1 st at outer edge on following 4th rows until there are 15 sts. Cont in Garter St until Collar measures approx 13 (13½, 13½, 14, 14)" ending with a WS row.
Next Row: Knit to last 3 sts, k2tog, k1. Knit 3 rows even. Rep last 4 rows until there are 11 sts, then dec 1 st at outer

bookworm tunic

photos on pages 82–83

SKILL LEVEL: Easy

SIZES: S (MEDIUM, L, XL)
Note: The pattern is written for the smallest size with changes for larger sizes in parentheses. When only one number is given, it applies to all sizes. For ease in working, before you begin, circle the numbers pertaining to the size you are knitting.

FINISHED MEASUREMENTS:
Bust: 37 (40, 43, 46)"
Length: 22½ (23, 23½, 24)"

MATERIALS:
Aurora Yarns, Giglio, 100% cotton, sport-weight yarn (88 yards per skein): 13 (14, 15, 16) balls of Cinnamon (984)
Size 6 (4 mm) knitting needles or size needed to obtain gauge
Size 5 (3.75 mm) knitting needles
1 stitch holder
Safety pin
Yarn needle

GAUGE:
In St st (knit RS rows, purl WS rows) with larger needles, 21 sts and 27 rows = 4"/10 cm.
TAKE TIME TO CHECK YOUR GAUGE.

edge on alt rows until there are 5 sts. Bind off (WS).
Collar Edging: With RS facing and crochet hook, join MC to outer edge of Collar. Work 1 row of sc across outer edge. Do not turn. Next Row: Ch 1, working from left to right, instead of from right to left, work 1 reverse sc in each sc across. Fasten off. Sew shoulder seams. Place markers on front edges 5½ (5½, 5½, 6, 6)" down from shoulder seams. Sew Collar in position between markers. Sew side and sleeve seams. Set in sleeves.
Cuff Edging: With RS facing and crochet hook, join MC at sleeve seam at top of Cuff. Work as for Collar Edging.
Outer Edging: Place 3 buttonhole markers on right front edge as follows: 5" above lower edge, ½" below beg of front shaping and in

center space between these 2 markers. Join MC with crochet hook at end of Collar on left front. Work 1 row of sc down left front, 3 sc in corner, sc across bottom of jacket and 3 sc in corner. Work up right front as follows: (Sc evenly to button marker, ch 2, skip ½" along front edge) 3 times, sc to end of collar. Do not turn.
Next Row: Ch 1, working from left to right, instead of from right to left, work 1 reverse sc in each sc and 2 reverse sc in each ch-2 sp across. Fasten off. Sew buttons in position on left front.

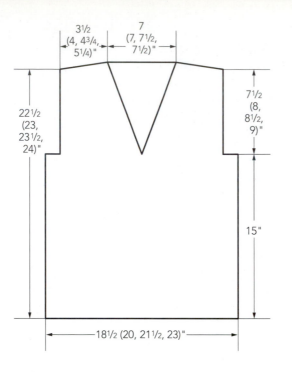

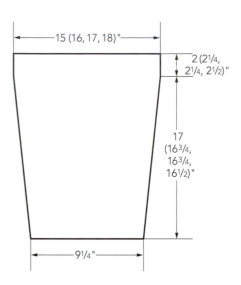

SPECIAL ABBREVIATIONS:

M1: Lift running thread before next stitch onto left-hand needle and knit in its back loop to make one stitch.

Ssk: Slip next 2 sts knitwise, one at a time to right-hand needle, insert tip of left-hand needle into fronts of these 2 sts and k them tog.

K2tog-b: Knit 2 sts together through the back loops.

STITCHES USED:

Eyelet Border (a multiple of 2 sts + 1 st; over 8 rows)

Rows 1–3: Knit, noting first row is WS.

Row 4 (RS): K1; * yo, k2tog, rep from * to end of row.

Rows 5–8: Purl.

These 8 rows form Eyelet Border

Dotted Check Pattern (a multiple of 8 sts + 1 st; a rep of 16 rows)

Row 1 (RS): Knit.

Row 2: Purl.

Row 3: K3; * p3, k5; rep from * to last 6 sts, p3, k3.

Row 4: P3; * k3, p5; rep from * to last 6 sts, k3, p3.

Row 5: K3; * p1, yo, p2tog, k5; rep from * to last 6 sts, p1, yo, p2tog, k3.

Row 6: As Row 4.

Row 7: As Row 3.

Row 8: Purl.

Row 9: Knit.

Row 10: Purl.

Row 11: K7; * p3, k5; rep from * across, ending p3, k7.

Row 12: P7; * k3, p5; rep from * across, ending k3, p7.

Row 13: K7; * p1, yo, p2tog, k5; rep from * across, ending p1, yo, p2tog, k7.

Row 14: As Row 12.

Row 15: As Row 11.

Row 16: Purl.

These 16 rows form Dotted Check Pat.

INSTRUCTIONS:
BACK

** Beg at lower edge with larger needles cast on 91 (99, 107, 115) sts. Work 8 rows of Eyelet Border.

Next Row (WS): Purl, inc 6 sts evenly across—97 (105, 113, 121) sts. Cont in St st for 21 more rows, ending with a knit row and dec 6 sts evenly across last row—91 (99, 107, 115) sts. Work 8 rows of Eyelet Border.

Next Row (WS): Purl, inc 6 sts evenly across—97 (105, 113, 121) sts. Work in Dotted Check Pat until piece from beg measures approx 15", ending with a WS row.

Armhole Shaping

Keeping cont of pat, bind off 11 (12, 12, 13) sts beg next 2 rows—75 (81, 89, 95) sts.** Cont even until piece measures approx 22½ (23, 23½, 24)" from beg, ending with a WS row.

Shoulder Shaping

Bind off 9 (11, 12, 14) sts beg next 2 rows, then 10 (11, 13, 14) sts beg following 2 rows. Leave rem 37 (37, 39, 39) sts on a st holder.

FRONT

Work from ** to ** as for Back.

V-Neck Shaping

Left Shoulder (RS): Pat across 34 (37, 41, 44) sts, ssk, k1 (neck edge); turn, leave rem sts on a spare needle. Work 1 row even in pat.
Next Row: Pat to last 3 sts, ssk, k1. Rep last 2 rows 8 (8, 10, 10) times more—27 (30, 32, 35) sts. Work 3 rows even in pat. **Next Row:** Pat to last 3 sts, ssk, k1. Rep last 4 rows 7 (7, 6, 6) times more—19 (22, 25, 28) sts.
Cont even in pat until piece measures same length as Back to beg of shoulder shaping, ending with a WS row.

Shoulder Shaping

Bind off 9 (11, 12, 14) sts beg next row. Work 1 row even. Bind off rem 10 (11, 13, 14) sts.
Right Shoulder: With RS of work facing, slip center st onto safety pin. Join yarn to rem sts and work to correspond to Left Shoulder, reversing all shapings by working k1, k2tog, at beg of neck-shaping rows.

SLEEVES (make two)

With larger needles cast on 49 sts. Work 8 rows of Eyelet Border.
Next Row (WS): Purl, inc 2 sts evenly across—51 sts. Cont in St st for 21 more rows, inc 1 st each edge of 5th row and following 6th rows twice—57 sts. Work 8 rows of Eyelet Border. Work in Dotted Check Pat for 4 rows. Keeping cont of pat, inc 1 st each edge NOW and every 6th row 10 (6, 5, 0) times then every 4th row 0 (7, 10, 17) times—79 (85, 89, 93) sts, taking inc sts into pat. Cont even in pat until sleeve measures approx 19" from beg, ending with a purl row. Bind off. Place markers on sides of sleeves 2 (2¼, 2¼, 2½)" down from bind off edge.

FINISHING

Sew right shoulder seam.
V-Neck Edging: With RS of work facing and smaller needles, pick up and knit 51 (53, 55, 57) sts down left front neck edge, k1 from front safety pin and mark as center st, pick up and knit 51 (53, 55, 57) sts up right front neck edge and k37 (37, 39, 39) from back st holder dec 3 sts evenly across—137 (141, 147, 151) sts.
Row 1 (WS): Knit to center 3 sts, k2tog-b, knit to end of row.
Row 2: Knit to center 3 sts, sl 1, k2tog, psso, knit to end of row.
Row 3: As Row 1.
Row 4: K1, * yo, k2tog, rep from * to end of row.
Row 5: Purl.
Rows 6 and 7: Purl to center 3 sts, p3tog, purl to end of row. Bind off purlwise (RS). Sew left shoulder and V-neck edging seam. Set in sleeves placing rows above markers along cast-off edges at armholes to form square armholes. Sew side and sleeve seams.

simply

Put on a sweater when your goals for the day are comfort and warmth. Knits breathe, stretch, and flow—wrapping you in softness that rivals any other clothing. This chapter brims with a variety of sweaters that are knit, crocheted, tied, cropped, cabled, bobbled, and buttoned. So grab your yarn and knitting needles to create a cozy sweater for yourself or someone you love.

cozy

TEXTURED PULLOVER

Knit with super-chunky weight yarn, this heather green sweater is laden with texture. The toasty top has set-in sleeves with ribbing that accents the neckline. Instructions begin on page 128.

comfy

SHAWL-COLLAR WRAP

If you enjoy working garter stitches, add this project to your want-to-make-it list. The variegated yarn beautifully accents the stitched stripes and the oversized style and wrap closure make the fit easy. Instructions begin on page 129.

warm

SNAZZY CROCHET COWL-NECK

Use yarn as soft as terry cloth to crochet
this attractive pale green cowl neck.
Raised stripes detail the entire sweater.
Instructions begin on page 131.

pastel

JAZZY JACKET

Easy-knit checked pockets and lapels classify this cardigan as a winner. Finish with split cuffs, raised edgings, and pretty buttons and you'll be right in style. Instructions begin on page 133.

classy

SEED-STITCH AND LACE BABY CARDIGAN

Dress your little honey like the angel she is in this lacy seed-stitch sweater. Knit with baby-soft acrylic yarn, the lace and upper-body stripe patterns are easy to master.

Instructions begin on page 137.

sweet

BUBBLE-GUM BABY

If your little gal wears sizes 2 through 8, she'll love this sweater that has a coordinating blankie for her baby doll! The sweater buttons at the shoulders through garter-stitch bands and the stripes at the lower hem are duplicated in rows across the blanket. Instructions begin on page 139.

adorable

TOTALLY TIED JACKET

Dotted details stand out brilliantly on this cream stockinette-stitch cardigan. A trio of ties finishes the dressy sweater jacket that is knit of acrylic and wool blend yarn. Instructions begin on page 141.

tied

BALLERINA-NECK SWEATER

Use cotton yarn with a touch of lycra to help this raspberry sweater keep its shape. Three-quarter-length sleeves, ballerina neckline, and open ribbing styling look pretty in any color. Instructions begin on page 144.

121

trendy

OFF TO BRUNCH

A trio of diamond patterns parades down the front of this wintry merino wool raglan sweater. To accent the silvery yarn, knitted white trim details the cowl neck and split cuffs. Instructions begin on page 146.

textured

SO-SOFT BABY SWEATER, BONNET, AND BOOTIES

Put a bonnet on your baby and she'll look as cute as a button. Add a matching sweater with easy square armholes and laced booties, and your little sweetheart will be irresistible! These soft crochets are full of lovely details, including a tiny waffle texture, dainty edges, and crocheted ties. Instructions begin on page 148.

crocheted

patterned

WEEKENDS UP NORTH

Extra long with side slits, this comfortable knit is made with wool and mohair yarn in khaki. The bodice has a rolled collar and pretty diamonds and bobbles. The lower portion and sleeves have stripes and knit-in chevrons. Instructions begin on page 151.

textured pullover

photos on pages 106–107

SKILL LEVEL: Easy

SIZES: XS (SMALL, M, L, XL, XXL)
Note: The pattern is written for the smallest size with changes for larger sizes in parentheses. *When only one number is given, it applies to all sizes. For ease in working, before you begin, circle the numbers pertaining to the size you are knitting.*

FINISHED MEASUREMENTS:
Chest: 39½ (43, 46, 50, 53½, 57)"
Length: 21 (22, 23, 24, 25, 26)"

MATERIALS:
Lion Brand, Wool-Ease Thick & Quick, Article 640, 80% acrylic/20% wool, super-chunky-weight yarn (108 yards per ball): 5 (6, 6, 7, 8, 9) balls of Green Heather (130)
Size 13 (9 mm) knitting needles or size needed to obtain gauge
Size 10½ (6.5 mm) circular knitting needle, 16-inch-length
Ring-type stitch marker
Four safety pins for markers
Yarn needle

GAUGE:
In Body Pattern with larger needles, 9 sts and 13 rows = 4"/10 cm.
TAKE TIME TO CHECK YOUR GAUGE.

STITCHES USED:
Body Pattern (a multiple of 2 sts + 1 st; a rep of 4 rows)
Row 1 (WS): P1; (k1, p1) across.
Row 2: K1; (p1, k1) across.
Row 3: Rep Row 1.
Row 4: Rep Row 1.
Rep Rows 1–4 for Body Pattern.

128

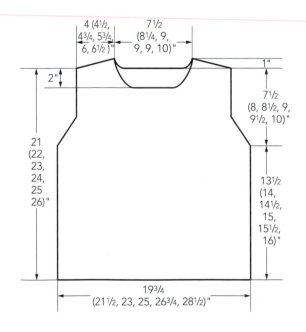

4 (4½, 4¾, 5¾, 6, 6½)"

7½ (8¼, 9, 9, 9, 10)"

1"

2"

7½ (8, 8½, 9, 9½, 10)"

21 (22, 23, 24, 25, 26)"

13½ (14, 14½, 15, 15½, 16)"

19¾ (21½, 23, 25, 26¾, 28½)"

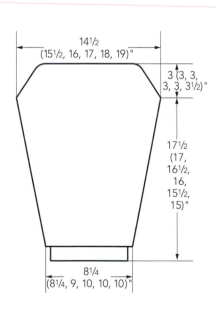

14½ (15½, 16, 17, 18, 19)"

3 (3, 3, 3, 3, 3½)"

17½ (17, 16½, 16, 15½, 15)"

8¼ (8¼, 9, 10, 10, 10)"

INSTRUCTIONS:
BACK
Beg at the lower edge with larger needles, cast on 45 (49, 53, 57, 61, 65) sts. Work Body Pat to approx 13½ (14, 14½, 15, 15½, 16)" from beg, ending with a WS row. Place a safety pin at each edge to mark beg of armhole.

Armhole Shaping
Working dec after first and before last sts, dec 1 st each edge every other row 5 (5, 5, 5, 5, 6) times—35 (39, 43, 47, 51, 53) sts. Continue in pat to approx 21 (22, 23, 24, 25, 26)" from beg, ending with a WS row.

Neck and Shoulder Shaping
Work pat on first 12 (13, 14, 16, 17, 18) sts, join 2nd ball of yarn and bind off center 11 (13, 15, 15, 17, 17) sts, pat to end. Working shoulders at the same time and with separate balls of yarn, bind off 5 (5, 6, 7, 7, 8) sts at each shoulder edge ONCE, then 4 (5, 5, 6, 7, 7) sts once. AT THE SAME TIME, bind off 3 sts at each neck edge once.

FRONT
Work as for Back to approx 19 (20, 21, 22, 23, 24)" from beg, ending with a WS row.

Neck Shaping
Work pat on first 14 (15, 16, 18, 19, 20) sts, join 2nd ball of yarn and bind off center 7 (9, 11, 11, 13, 13) sts, pat to end of row. Working shoulders at the same time and with separate balls of yarn, bind off 2 sts at each neck edge once. Dec 1 st at each neck edge 3 times— 9 (10, 11, 13, 14, 15) sts rem.

When piece measures same as Back to shoulder, shape shoulders as for Back.

SLEEVES (make two)
Beg at the lower edge with smaller needles, cast on 19 (19, 21, 23, 23, 23) sts. Work Body Pat for 1½". Change to larger needles and continue in pat. Including new sts into pat as they accumulate, inc 1 st each edge every 4th row 0 (0, 1, 2, 6, 10) time(s) then every 6th row 7 (8, 7, 6, 3, 0) times. Continue in pat on 33 (35, 37, 39, 41, 43) sts to approx 17½ (17, 16½, 16, 15½, 15)" from beg.

Sleeve Cap Shaping
Working dec after first and before last sts, dec 1 st each edge every other row 5 (5, 5, 5, 5, 6) times—23 (25, 27, 29, 31, 31) sts. Bind off 2 sts at the beg of the next 2 rows. Bind off rem 19 (21, 23, 25, 27, 27) sts.

FINISHING:
Join shoulder seams. Set in sleeves. Join underarm and side seams.
Neckband
With the RS facing and circular needle, beg at one shoulder seam of neck edge pick up and k42 (46, 50, 50, 54, 54) sts evenly spaced around neck. Place marker to indicate beg of rnd.
Rnd 1: (K1, p1) around.
Rnds 2–4: (P1, k1) around.
Rnd 5: Rep Rnd 1.
In est Rnd 1 pat, bind off all sts.

shawl-collar wrap
photos on pages 108–109

SKILL LEVEL: Easy

SIZES: SMALL (M, L, XL, XXL)
Note: The pattern is written for the smallest size with changes for larger sizes in parentheses. When only one number is given, it applies to all sizes. For ease in working, before you begin, circle the numbers pertaining to the size you are knitting.

FINISHED MEASUREMENTS:
Bust: 41 (45, 49, 53, 57)"
Back Length: 22½ (23, 23½, 24, 24½)"

MATERIALS:
Muench Yarns, Naturwolle, 100% wool, bulky weight yarn (100 meters per ball): 10 (12, 13, 14, 16) balls of Madagaskar (100)
Size 11 (8 mm) knitting needles or size needed to obtain gauge
Size 11 (8 mm) 29"-length circular knitting needles
Two ring-type stitch markers
Yarn needle

GAUGE:
In Garter St (knit every row), 12 sts and 22 rows = 4"/10 cm
TAKE TIME TO CHECK YOUR GAUGE.

SPECIAL ABBREVIATIONS:
Ssk: Slip next 2 sts knitwise, one at a time to right-hand needle, insert tip of left-hand needle into fronts of these 2 sts and k them together.

Armhole Shaping
Bind off 2 sts at beg of next 2 rows.
Dec Row 1 (RS): K1, ssk, k across, ending k2tog, k1.
Row 2: P1, k across, ending p1. Rep last 2 rows 3 (5, 6, 7, 9) times more. Keeping 1 st each edge in St st (knit RS rows, purl WS rows), work even on 50 (52, 56, 60, 62) sts until piece measures approx 22½ (23, 23½, 24, 24½)" from beg, ending with a WS row. Place markers either side of center 10 (12, 14, 14, 16) sts.

Shoulder and Neck Shaping
Bind off 3 sts at beg of next 2 rows. Next Row: Bind off 3 (3, 3, 4, 4) sts, k to marker, join a new ball of yarn and bind off center 10 (12, 14, 14, 16) sts, k to end of row. Next Row: Bind off 3 (3, 3, 4, 4) sts, k to end. Working shoulders at the same time and with separate balls, bind off 3 (3, 4, 4, 4) sts EACH shoulder edge once and 4 sts EACH shoulder edge twice.

M1: Lift running thread before next stitch onto left-hand needle and knit in its back loop to make one stitch.

Note: Fronts and Back are different lengths.

INSTRUCTIONS:
BACK
Cast on 62 (68, 74, 80, 86) sts. Work in Garter Stitch Body Pattern:
All Rows: Slip first st as if to k, k across. Continue in pattern until piece measures approx 14½" from beg.

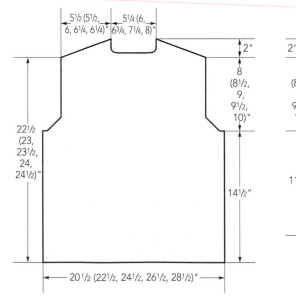

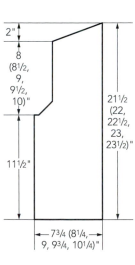

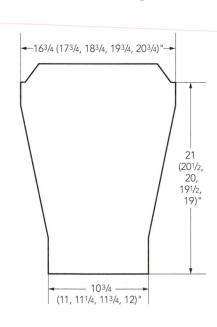

AT SAME TIME, bind off 2 (2, 2, 3, 3) sts EACH neck edge once and 1 st EACH neck edge once.

RIGHT FRONT
Cast on 23 (25, 27, 29, 31) sts. Work Garter Stitch Body Pattern as for Back until piece measures approx 11½" from beg, ending with a RS row.
Armhole Shaping
Bind off 2 sts at beg of next row. **Dec Row (RS):** K across to last 3 sts, k2tog, k1. **Next Row:** P1, k across. Rep last 2 rows 3 (5, 6, 7, 9) times more. Keeping 1 st at armhole edge in St st, work even on 17 (17, 18, 19, 19) sts until piece measures approx 19½ (20, 20½, 21, 21½)" from beg, ending with a RS row.
Shoulder Shaping
Bind off 3 sts at shoulder edge on next row and every other row 2 (2, 1, 0, 0) time(s) more, then bind off 4 sts from shoulder edge every other row 2 (2, 3, 4, 4) times.

LEFT FRONT
Work as for Right Front reversing all shaping.

SLEEVES (make two)
Cast on 32 (33, 34, 35, 36) sts. Work Garter Stitch Body Pattern as for Back to approx 4" from beg. **Inc Row (RS):** Slip 1, M1, k across to last st, M1, k1. Inc 1 st each edge every 6th row 0 (0, 1, 6, 12) time(s), then every 8th row 0 (5, 9, 5, 0) times, then every 10th row 8 (4, 0, 0, 0) times. Work even in pattern on 50 (53, 56, 59, 62) sts until piece measures approx 21 (20½, 20, 19½, 19)" total from beg, ending with a WS row.

Sleeve Cap Shaping
Bind off 2 sts at beg of next 2 rows. **Dec Row 1 (RS):** K1, ssk, k across, ending k2tog, k1. Row 2: P1, k across, ending p1. Rep last 2 rows 3 (5, 6, 8, 9) times more. Bind off rem 38 (37, 38, 37, 38) sts on next RS row.

FINISHING
Block pieces to measurements. Sew shoulder seams. Set in sleeves. Sew sleeve seams, reversing front/back of seam at bottom 2". Sew side seams leaving bottom 4" of front and 7½" of back free for side slits.
Shawl Collar
With RS facing and circular needle, beg at bottom of right front edge. Skip first 3", pick up and k55 (56, 57, 59, 60) sts evenly across the rem 18 (18½, 19, 19½, 20)" to shoulder of Front edge. Pick up and k20 (22, 24, 26, 28) sts evenly across back neck, pick up and k55 (56, 57, 59, 60) sts evenly across top 18 (18½, 19, 19½, 20)" of Left Front edge leaving rem 3" of lower edge free—130 (134, 138, 144, 148) sts. Work Garter St as follows (all rows): Slip first st as if to k, k across. Work until piece measures approx 6 (6½, 7, 7½, 8)" from beg. Bind off loosely.

snazzy crochet cowl-neck

photos on pages 110–111

SKILL LEVEL: Easy

SIZES: S (MEDIUM, L, XL)
Note: The pattern is written for the smallest size with changes for larger sizes in parentheses. When only one number is given, it applies to all sizes. For ease in working, before you begin, circle the numbers pertaining to the size you are crocheting.

FINISHED MEASUREMENTS:
Bust: 34 (38, 42½, 47)"
Length: 20 (20½, 21, 21½)"

MATERIALS:
Coats & Clark, Red Heart Baby Teri, 52% acrylic/48% nylon, worsted-weight yarn (3 ounces per skein): 6 (7, 8, 9) skeins of Mint (9180)
Size I/9 (5.5 mm) crochet hook or size needed to obtain gauge
Yarn needle

GAUGE:
In Body Pattern, 16 sts and 20 rows = 5"/12.7 cm.
TAKE TIME TO CHECK YOUR GAUGE.

SPECIAL ABBREVIATIONS:
FPdc (front post double crochet): Yo, insert hook from front to back then to front to go around dc post, draw up a lp, (yo and draw through 2 lps on hook) twice.
Sc2tog: Draw up a lp in each of next 2 sts, yo and draw through all 3 lps on hook.

Sc3tog: Draw up a lp in each of next 3 sts, yo and draw through all 4 lps on hook.

Note: *Skip the sc behind each FPdc.*

STITCHES USED:
Body Pattern (a multiple of 7 sts + 5 sts; a rep of 2 rows)
Row 1 (RS): Ch 1, sc in first 2 sc; * FPdc over FPdc, sc in each of next 6 sc; rep from * across, ending FPdc over FPdc, sc in each of last 2 sc; turn.
Row 2: Ch 1, sc in each st across; turn.
Rep Rows 1–2 for Body Pattern.

INSTRUCTIONS:
BACK
Beg at lower edge and above the border, ch 55 (62, 69, 76).
Foundation Row (RS): Sc in 2nd ch from hook and in next ch; * ch 1, sk 1 ch, sc in each of next 6 ch; rep from * across, ending ch 1, sk 1 ch, sc in last 2 ch—54 (61, 68, 75) sts; turn.
Row 2: Ch 1, sc in each st across; turn.

Row 3: Ch 1, sc in first 2 sc; * dc in skipped ch 2 rows below, sc in each of next 6 sc; rep from * across, ending dc in skipped ch 2 rows below, sc in each of last 2 sc; turn.
Row 4: As Row 2.
Row 5: Ch 1, sc in first 2 sc; * FPdc over dc, sc in each of next 6 sc. Rep from * across, ending FPdc over dc, sc in each of last 2 sc; turn.
Row 6: As Row 2.
Beg Body Pattern and work to approx 12" from beg, ending with a WS row.

Armhole Shaping
Sl st in first sc, in next sc (sl st, ch 1, sc); work est pattern across, ending with skip last sc; turn. **Next Row:** Ch 1, sc2tog, pattern across, ending sc2tog; turn. Rep last row 5 (8, 10, 13) times more. Work even on rem 40 (41, 44, 45) sts until piece measures approx 19½ (20, 20½, 21)" from beg, ending with a RS row. Fasten off.

FRONT
Work as for Back until piece measures approx 17 (17½, 18, 18½)" from beg, ending with a WS row.
Left Shoulder
Pattern across first 11 (11, 13, 13) sts; turn. Ch 1, sc2tog, pattern to end; turn. Pattern across, ending sc2tog; turn. Ch 1, sc2tog, pattern to end; turn. Work even on rem 8 (8, 10, 10) sts until piece measures approx 19½ (20, 20½, 21)" from beg, ending with a RS row. Fasten off.

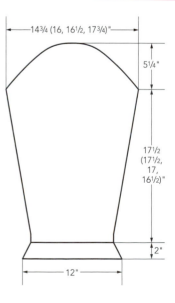

Right Shoulder

With RS facing, skip center 18 (19, 18, 19) sts for front neck, join yarn with sl st in next st, sc in same st as join, pattern to end. Dec 1 st at neck edge every row 3 times. Complete as for Left Shoulder.

SLEEVES (make two)

Beg at lower edge and above the cuff, ch 32.

Foundation Row (RS): Sc in 2nd ch from hook; * ch 1, sk 1 ch, sc in each of next 6 ch; rep from * across, ending ch 1, sk 1 ch, sc in last ch—31 sts; turn.

Row 2: Ch 1, sc in each st across; turn.

Row 3: Ch 1, sc in first sc; * dc in skipped ch 2 rows below, sc in each of next 6 sc; rep from * across, ending dc in skipped ch 2 rows below, sc in last sc; turn.

Row 4: As Row 2.

Row 5: Ch 1, 2 sc in first sc; * FPdc over dc, sc in each of next 6 sc; rep from * across, ending FPdc over dc, 2 sc in last sc—33 sts; turn.

Row 6: As Row 2.

Beg Body Pattern. Including new sts into Body Pattern as they accumulate, inc 1 st each edge every 4th row 0 (0, 3, 10) times and every 6th row 7 (9, 7, 2) times. Work even on 47 (51, 53, 57) sts to approx 17½ (17½, 17, 16½)" from beg, ending with a WS row.

Sleeve Cap Shaping

Sl st in first st, in next st (sl st, ch 1, sc), pattern across, skipping last st. Dec 1 st each edge every other row 5 times then every row 5 times. Ch 1, sc3tog, pattern to last 3 sts, sc3tog; turn. Rep last row twice more. **Last RS Row:** Ch 1, sc2tog, pattern across, ending sc2tog—11 (15, 17, 21) sts. Fasten off.

FINISHING

Join shoulder seams.

Cowl Neck

WS facing, beg at center of back neck, work 60 sc evenly spaced around neck; join with sl st in first sc.

Rnd 2: Ch 1, sc in first 3 sc; * ch 1, sk 1 sc, sc in next 3 sc; rep from * around, ending ch 1, sk 1 sc, join with sl st in first sc.

Rnd 3: As Rnd 2.

Rnd 4: Ch 1, sc in first 3 sc; * dc in skipped sc 2 rows below, sc in next 3 sc; rep from * around, ending dc in skipped sc 2 rows below; join.

Rnd 5: Ch 1, sc in first 3 sc; * FPdc over dc, sc in next 3 sc; rep from * around, ending FPdc over dc; join.

Rnds 6–8: Ch 1, sc in first 3 sc; * FPdc over FPdc, sc in next 3 sc; rep from * around, ending FPdc over FPdc; join.

Rnd 9: Ch 1; * 2 sc in sc, sc in next sc, 2 sc in next sc, FPdc over FPdc; rep from * around; join.

Rnds 10–15: Ch 1; * sc in 5 sc, FPdc over FPdc; rep from * around; join.

Rnd 16: Ch 1, sc in same sc as join; * ch 2, working from left to right rather than right to left as is the norm, sk 1 sc, sc in next sc; rep from * around, ending ch 2, join with sl st in first ch-2 sp.

Rnds 17–20: Ch 1, sc in same ch-2 sp as join; * ch 2, sc in next ch-2 sp; rep from * around, ending ch 2, join with sl st in first ch-2 sp. After Rnd 20, fasten off.

Sleeve Borders (make two)

With RS facing, join yarn with sl st in first rem ch from Foundation at lower edge. Ch 1, (sc2tog), sc in each rem ch across—30 sts; join with sl st in first st. Work Rnds 16–20 as for Cowl Neck. **Last Rnd:** * In ch-2 sp (sl st, sc, sl st); rep from * around. Fasten off. Set in sleeves. Join underarm and side seams.

Lower Edging

With RS facing, sc in each rem ch from Foundation around, beg at a side seam; join. Ch 1, sc in same sc as join. For Reverse Sc; (ch 2, going left to right, sk 1 sc, sc in next sc) around, ending ch 2, sl st in first ch-2 sp. Fasten off.

jazzy jacket

photos on pages 112–113

SKILL LEVEL: Experienced

SIZES: XS (S, MEDIUM, L, XL)

Note: The pattern is written for the smallest size with changes for larger sizes in parentheses. When only one number is given, it applies to all sizes. For ease in working, circle the numbers pertaining to the size you are knitting.

FINISHED MEASUREMENTS:
Bust (buttoned): 36 (38, 40, 42, 44)"
Length: 22 (22½, 23, 23½, 24)"

MATERIALS:
Classic Elite, Beatrice, 100% merino wool, bulky-weight yarn (63 yards per ball): 16 (17, 18, 20, 21) balls of Fall Tweed (3285)
Size 10 (6 mm) knitting needles or size needed to obtain gauge

Size 9 (5 mm) knitting
  needles
Size 8 (5 mm) knitting
  needles; yarn needle
Size H/8 (5 mm) crochet hook
JHB International buttons,
  70258 Luminosity, one
  1"-diameter and four
  ¾"-diameter

134

GAUGE:
In St st (knit RS rows, purl WS
rows) with largest needles, 15
sts and 20 rows = 4"/10 cm.
TAKE TIME TO CHECK YOUR
GAUGE.

SPECIAL ABBREVIATIONS:
Ssk: Slip next 2 sts knitwise,
one at a time to right-hand
needle, insert tip of left-hand
needle into fronts of these
2 sts and k them tog.
M1: Lift running thread
before next stitch onto left-
hand needle and knit in its
back loop to make one stitch.
K-inc: Knit in front and back
of next stitch.

*Note: Crochet trim on all
outside edges is not reflected
on the schematic.*

INSTRUCTIONS:
BACK
Beg at lower edge with largest
needles, cast on 67 (71, 75, 79,
83) sts. Beg with a purl row,
work St st to approx 3" from
beg, ending with a WS row.
Side Shaping
Dec Row: K1, ssk, k across,
ending k2tog, k1. Work 3
rows even. Rep last 4 rows
twice more—61 (65, 69, 73,
77) sts. Work even to approx
8½" from beg, ending with a
WS row. **Inc Row:** K1, M1, k
across, ending M1, k1. Work
3 rows even. Rep last 4 rows
twice more—67 (71, 75, 79,
83) sts. Work even to approx
13½" from beg, ending with
a WS row.
Armhole Shaping
Bind off 4 sts at beg of next
2 rows. **Dec Row:** K1, ssk, k
across, ending k2tog, k1.
Purl next row. Rep last 2
rows 6 (6, 6, 7, 7) times more.
Work even on 45 (49, 53, 55,
59) sts to approx 21 (21½, 22,
22½, 23)" from beg, ending
with a WS row.

Shoulder and Neck Shaping
Bind off 5 (6, 7, 7, 8) sts each
shoulder edge once and 6 (7,
8, 8, 9) each shoulder edge
once. On next RS row, bind
off rem 23 (23, 23, 25, 25) sts.

RIGHT FRONT
Beg at lower edge with
largest needles, cast on 33
(35, 37, 39, 41) sts. Beg with
a purl row, work St st to
approx 3" from beg, ending
with a WS row.
Side Shaping
Dec Row: K across, ending
k2tog, k1. Work 3 rows even.
Rep last 4 rows twice more—
30 (32, 34, 36, 38) sts. Work
even to approx 8½" from
beg, ending with a WS row.
Inc Row: K across, ending
M1, k1. Work 3 rows even.
Rep last 4 rows twice more—
33 (35, 37, 39, 41) sts. Work
even to approx 12 (12½, 13,
13, 13¼)" from beg, ending
with a WS row.
Lapel (*Note:* When piece
measures approx 13½", end
with a RS row and go to
Armhole Shaping).
Row 1 (RS): Cast on 4 sts, k2,
p2 across new sts, k to end.
Row 2: P across, ending k3,
k-inc. **Row 3:** P1, k2, p2, k to
end. **Row 4:** P across,
ending k4, k-inc. **Row 5:** K2,
p2, k2, k to end. **Row 6:** P
across, ending k5, k-inc. **Row
7:** P1, k2, p2, k2, k to end. **Row
8:** P across, ending k6,
k-inc. **Row 9:** (K2, p2) twice,
k to end. **Row 10:** P across,
ending k7, k-inc. **Row 11:**
P1, (k2, p2) twice, k to end.
Row 12: P across, ending k8,
k-inc. **Row 13:** (K2, p2)
twice, k2, k to end. **Row 14:**
P across, ending k9, k-inc.
Row 15: P1, (k2, p2) twice,
k2, k to end. **Row 16:** P

across, ending k10, k-inc. **Row 17:** (K2, p2) 3 times, k to end. **Row 18:** P across, ending k11, k-inc. **Row 19:** P1, (k2, p2) 3 times, k to end. **Row 20:** P across, ending k12, k-inc. **Row 21:** (K2, p2) 3 times, k2, k to end. **Row 22:** P across, ending k13, k-inc. **Row 23:** P1, (k2, p2) 3 times, k2, k to end. **Row 24:** P across, ending k14, k-inc. **Row 25:** (K2, p2) 4 times, k to end. **Row 26:** P across, ending k15, k-inc. **Row 27:** P1, (k2, p2) 4 times, k to end. **Row 28:** P across, ending k16, k-inc. **Row 29:** (K2, p2) 4 times, k2, k to end. **Row 30 (Sizes XS, S, M):** P across, ending k18; go to Neck Shaping. **Row 30 (Sizes L & XL):** P across, ending k17, k-inc. **Row 31:** P1, (k2, p2) 4 times, k2, k to end. **Row 32 (Size L):** P across, ending k19; go to Neck Shaping. **Row 32 (Size XL):** P across, ending k18, k-inc. **Row 33:** (K2, p2) 5 times, k to end. **Row 34:** P across, ending k20; go to **Neck Shaping**.

Armhole Shaping
When piece measures approx 13½" from beg, end with a RS row. Bind off 4 sts at beg of next row. **Dec Row:** Pattern across, ending k2tog, k1. Rep Dec Row every RS row 6 (6, 6, 7, 7) times more.

Neck Shaping
With RS facing, bind off first 23 (23, 23, 24, 24) sts, placing a marker on last st. K to end—17 (19, 21, 22, 25) sts. At neck edge every other row, bind off 3 sts once, 2 sts once, and 1 st 1 (1, 1, 2, 3) time(s). Work even on rem 11 (13, 15, 15, 17) sts to approx 21 (21½, 22, 22½, 23)" from beg, ending with a RS row.

Shoulder Shaping
At shoulder edge, bind off 5 (6, 7, 7, 8) sts once and 6 (7, 8, 8, 9) sts once.

LEFT FRONT
Work as for Right Front to Side Shaping. **Dec Row:** K1, ssk, k across. Work 3 rows even. Rep last 4 rows twice more—30 (32, 34, 36, 38) sts. Work even to approx 8½"

from beg, ending with a WS row. **Inc Row:** K1, M1, k to end. Work 3 rows even. Rep last 4 rows twice more—33 (35, 37, 39, 41) sts. Work even to approx 12 (12½, 13, 13, 13¼)" from beg, ending with a WS row.

Lapel (***Note:*** When piece measures approx 13½", end with a WS row and go to Armhole Shaping).
Row 1 (RS): K across, ending cast on 4 sts. **Row 2:** K4, p to end. **Row 3:** K across, ending p2, k2. **Row 4:** K-inc, k3, p to end. **Row 5:** K across, ending k2, p2, k1. **Row 6:** K-inc, k4, p to end. **Row 7:** K across, ending k2, p2, k2. **Row 8:** K-inc, k5, p to end. **Row 9:** K across, ending p2, k2, p2, k1. **Row 10:** K-inc, k6, p to end. **Row 11:** K across, ending (p2, k2) twice. **Row 12:** K-inc, k7, p to end. **Row 13:** K across, ending (k2, p2) twice, k1. **Row 14:** K-inc, k8, p to end. **Row 15:** K across, ending (k2, p2) twice, k2. **Row 16:** K-inc, k9, p to end. **Row 17:** K across, ending

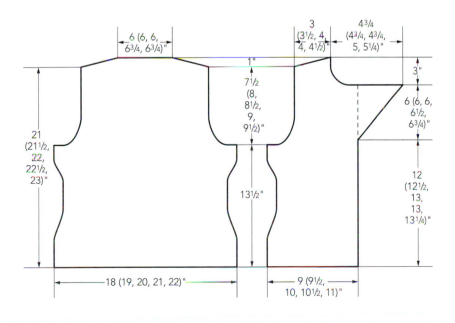

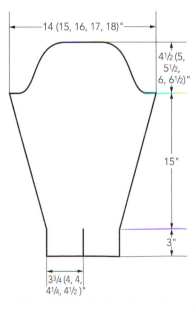

(p2, k2) twice, p2, k1. **Row 18:** K-inc, k10, p to end. **Row 19:** K across, ending (p2, k2) 3 times. **Row 20:** K-inc, k11, p to end. **Row 21:** K across, ending (k2, p2) 3 times, k1. **Row 22:** K-inc, k12, p to end. **Row 23:** K across, ending (k2, p2) 3 times, k2. **Row 24:** K-inc, k13, p to end. **Row 25:** K across, ending (p2, k2) 3 times, p2, k1. **Row 26:** K-inc, k14, p to end. **Row 27:** K across, ending (p2, k2) 4 times. **Row 28:** K-inc, k15, p to end. **Row 29:** K across, ending (k2, p2) 4 times, k1. **Row 30:** K-inc, k16, p to end. **Row 31:** K across, ending (k2, p2) 4 times, k2. (Sizes XS, S, M—go to Neck Shaping). **Row 32 (Sizes L & XL):** K-inc, k17, p to end. **Row 33:** K across, ending (p2, k2) 4 times, p2, k1. Size L—go to Neck Shaping. **Row 34:** K-inc, k18, p to end. **Row 35:** K across, ending (p2, k2) 5 times.

Armhole Shaping

Bind off 4 sts, work to end. **Dec Row:** K1, ssk, pattern across. Rep Dec Row every RS row for 6 (6, 6, 7, 7) times more.

Neck Shaping

With WS facing, bind off first 23 (23, 23, 24, 24) sts—placing a marker on last st—17 (19, 21, 23, 25) sts. Reversing shaping, complete as for Right Front.

SLEEVES (make two)

Beg at lower edge with largest needles, cast on 14 (15, 15, 16, 17) sts. With a new ball of yarn, cast on 14 (15, 15, 16, 17) sts. Working sides separately and at the same time, beg with a purl row, work St st to approx 3"

from beg, ending with a RS row. Next Row: Purl across all sts; leaving a tail to weave in later, cut second ball of yarn. **Inc Row:** K1, M1, k across, ending M1, k1. Rep Inc Row every 4th row 0 (3, 9, 13, 16) times more then every 6th row 11 (9, 5, 2, 0) times. Work even on 52 (56, 60, 64, 68) sts to approx 18" from beg, ending with a WS row.

Sleeve Cap Shaping

Bind off 4 sts at beg of next 2 rows. **Dec Row:** K1, ssk, k across, ending k2tog, k1. Purl next row. Rep last 2 rows 6 (6, 6, 7, 7) times more —30 (34, 38, 40, 44) sts. Work 0 (2, 4, 6, 8) rows even. Bind off 2 (3, 4, 4, 5) sts twice, 3 (3, 4, 4, 5) sts twice, and 3 (4, 4, 5, 5) sts twice. Bind off rem 14 sts.

POCKETS (make two)

Beg at top edge, with largest needles, cast on 18 sts. **Row 1 (WS):** K2; (p2, k2) across. **Row 2:** Knit. **Row 3–4:** As Rows 1–2. **Row 5:** P2; (k2, p2) across. **Row 6:** Knit. **Rows 7–8:** As Rows 5–6. Rep Rows 1–8 for 3 times total. On last 4 rows, dec 1 st each edge on rows 6 and 8. Bind off 14 sts. With crochet hook, sc around entire pocket. Slip stitch in each sc around. Working between slip stitches from previous rnd, sl st around and fasten off. Sew small button in center, 1½" from top edge.

FINISHING

Join shoulder seams.
Collar
With RS of jacket facing, beg at Right Front marker, with smallest needles, pick up and

k24 (24, 24, 25, 25) sts to shoulder, 22 (22, 22, 24, 24) sts along back neck, and 24 (24, 24, 25, 25) sts from shoulder to Left Front marker —70 (70, 70, 74, 74) sts. **Row 1 (RS of Collar):** Knit. **Row 2:** (K2, p2) across, ending k2. **Rows 3–4:** Rep Rows 1–2. **Row 5:** Knit. **Row 6:** (P2, k2) across, ending p2. **Rows 7–8:** Rep Rows 5–6. Change to middle-size needles and rep Rows 1–4. Change to largest needles and rep Rows 5–6. **Row 15:** K-inc, k across, ending k-inc. **Row 16:** K1; (p2, k2) across, ending p2, k1. **Row 17:** Knit. **Row 18:** P1; (k2, p2) across, ending k2, p1. **Row 19:** As Row 15. **Row 20:** P2; (k2, p2) across. Bind off all sts loosely and knitwise.

Front Band and Lower Edging

With RS facing, using crochet hook, join yarn with a slip st beneath the lapel on left front. Ch 1, sc evenly to corner, 3 sc in corner, sc along lower edge and work 3 sc in corner, sc to next lapel; turn. **Row 2:** Ch 1, sc in first sc, ch 2, sk 2 sc for buttonhole, sc in each sc around; turn. **Row 3:** Ch 1, sc in each sc around, working 3 sc in each corner and 2 sc over ch-2 sp; turn. **Row 4:** Slip st in each sc around; turn. **Row 5:** Working beneath the slip sts from previous row, sl st around and fasten off. Sew large button opposite buttonhole. Set in sleeves. Join underarm and side seams.

Sleeve Edging (make two)
With RS facing, using crochet hook, join yarn with a sl st in seam of lower sleeve. Ch 1, sc evenly along sleeve and on each side of vent, working 3 sc in each of the 2 corners.
Rnd 2: Sl st in first sc and in each sc around.
Rnd 3: Working beneath the sl sts from previous row, slip stitch around and fasten off. Sew a small button above each sleeve vent.
Pin pockets onto fronts, 2" from front edges and 2" from lower edge. Sew in place.

Lapel and Collar Edging
With RS facing, using crochet hook, join yarn with a sl st at base of left front lapel. Ch 1, sc evenly around lapel, collar and lapel, working 3 sc in each corner; turn. **Row 2:** Sl st in each sc around.
Row 3: Working beneath the sl sts from previous row, sl stitch around and fasten off.

seed-stitch and lace baby cardigan

photos on pages 114–115

SKILL LEVEL: Intermediate

SIZES: Infants SIX (12, 18) months

Note: *The pattern is written for the smallest size with changes for larger sizes in parentheses. When only one number is given, it applies to all sizes. For ease in working, before you begin, circle the numbers pertaining to the size you are knitting.*

FINISHED MEASUREMENTS:
Chest (buttoned): 24 (26, 28)"
Length: 11 (12, 13)"

MATERIALS:
Coats & Clark, Red Heart Soft Baby, 100% acrylic, sport-weight yarn (7 ounces per skein): For all sizes, 1 skein of Powder Yellow (7321)
Size 6 (4 mm) knitting needles or size needed to obtain gauge
2 stitch holders
Three ½" buttons
Tapestry needle

GAUGE:
In Body Pattern, 24 sts and 30 rows = 4"/10 cm.
TAKE TIME TO CHECK YOUR GAUGE.

SPECIAL ABBREVIATIONS
K1b: Knit next stitch in the back loop.

STITCHES USED:
Seed Stitch (a multiple of 2 sts + 1 st; a rep of 1 row)
Row 1: P1; (k1, p1) across. Rep Row 1 for Seed St.

Lace Pattern (a multiple of 6 sts + 1 st; a rep of 4 rows)
Row 1 (WS): * P1, k1, p3, k1; rep from * across, ending p1.
Row 2: * K1b, p1, yo, p3tog, yo, p1; rep from * across, ending k1b.
Row 3: As Row 1.
Row 4: * K1b, (p1, k1) twice, p1; rep from * across, ending k1b.
Rep Rows 1–4 for Lace Pattern.

Body Pattern (a multiple of 6 sts + 1 st; a rep of 2 rows)
Row 1 (WS): P1; (k1, p1) across.
Row 2: * K1b, p2, k1, p2; rep from * across, ending k1b.
Rep Rows 1–2 for Body Pattern.

INSTRUCTIONS:
BACK
Beg at lower edge, cast on 71 (77, 83) sts. Work Seed St to approx 1" from beg.

Set Up for Lace Pattern
Row 1 (WS): Seed St over 2 sts; Row 1 of Lace Pattern across, ending Seed St over

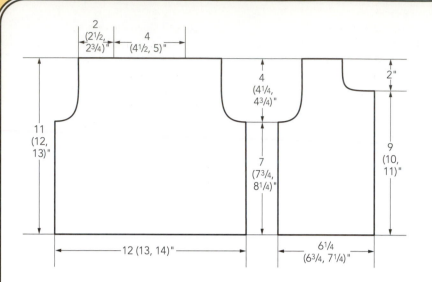

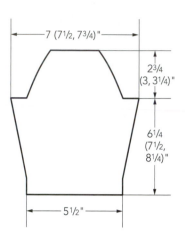

last 2 sts. Pattern is now set. Cont as est to approx 6" from beg, ending with Row 2. Beg Body Pattern keeping 2 sts at each edge in Seed St and work to approx 7 (7¾, 8¼)" from beg, ending with a WS row.

Armhole Shaping
Bind off 6 sts at beg of next 2 rows. Dec 1 st each edge every other row 3 (4, 5) times. Keeping 2 sts each edge in Seed St, work even on rem 53 (57, 61) sts to approx 11 (12, 13)" from beg, ending with a WS row. Bind off knitwise.

LEFT FRONT
Beg at lower edge, cast on 37 (39, 43) sts. Work Seed St to approx 1" from beg, inc 1 st in center of last row—38 (40, 44) sts.

Set Up for Lace Pattern Row 1 (WS): Seed St over 5 (7, 5) sts, Row 1 of Lace Pattern across, ending Seed St over last 2 sts.
Pattern is now set. Cont as est to approx 6" from beg, ending with Row 2. Beg Body Pattern keeping Seed St as est, and work to approx

7 (7¾, 8¼)" from beg, ending with a WS row.

Armhole Shaping
Bind off 6 sts at beg of next row. Dec 1 st at armhole edge every other row 3 (4, 5) times. Keeping 2 sts at armhole edge in Seed St, work even on rem 29 (30, 33) sts to approx 9 (10, 11)" from beg, ending with a RS row.

Neck Shaping
Work Seed St over first 5 sts and place on a holder, bind off next 3 (4, 6) sts. At neck edge, bind off 3 sts once, 2 sts once, and 1 st once. Work even on rem 15 (15, 16) sts to same length as Back, ending with a WS row. Bind off knitwise. Place markers for two buttonholes with the first 4 (5, 6)" from lower edge and the second 2½" from neck edge.

RIGHT FRONT
Cast on and work Seed St as for Left Front.

Set Up for Lace Pattern Row 1 (WS): Seed St over 2 sts, Row 1 of Lace Pattern across, ending Seed St over 5 (7, 5) sts.
Pattern is now set. Work as for Left Front, reversing

armhole and neck shaping. When piece measures approx 4 (5, 6)" from beg, end with a WS row. **Buttonhole Row:** Seed St over first 2 sts, yo, work 2 sts tog, pat to end of row. Rep Buttonhole Row to correspond to second marker on Left Front.

SLEEVES (make two)
Beg at lower edge, cast on 33 sts. Work Seed St to approx 1" from beg, ending with a RS row.

Set Up for Body Pattern Row 1 (WS): Seed St over 1 st, Row 1 of Body Pattern across, ending Seed St over 1 st.
Including new sts into Seed St as they accumulate, inc 1 st each edge every 8th row 4 (6, 7) times. Work even on 41 (45, 47) sts to approx 6¼ (7½, 8¼)" from beg, ending with a WS row.

Sleeve Cap Shaping
Bind off 6 (4, 4) sts at beg of next 2 rows. Dec 1 st each edge every other row until 19 sts rem. Dec 1 st each edge every row, twice. Bind off rem 15 sts.

FINISHING

Join shoulder seams. Set in sleeves. Join underarm and side seams.

Neckband

With RS facing, beg at right front, join yarn and work Seed St across 5 sts from holder. Pick up and k 17 sts evenly spaced to shoulder, 23 (27, 29) sts along back neck and 17 sts evenly spaced along left front, Seed St across 5 sts from holder—67 (71, 73) sts. Work Seed St across next row. **Buttonhole Row:** Seed St over first 2 sts, yo, work 2 sts tog, work to end of row. Work 3 additional Seed St rows. Bind off in Seed St. Sew buttons opposite buttonholes.

bubble-gum baby

photos on pages 116–117

SKILL LEVEL: Easy

SIZES: Children's size 2 (FOUR, 6, 8)
Note: The pattern is written for the smallest size with changes for larger sizes in parentheses. When only one number is given, it applies to all sizes. For ease in working, before you begin, circle the numbers pertaining to the size you are knitting.

FINISHED MEASUREMENTS:
Chest: 26 (29½, 31½, 33½)"
Length: 13 (15, 16, 18)"

MATERIALS:
Lion Brand, Cotton-Ease, 50% cotton/50% acrylic, worsted-weight yarn (207 yards per skein). For Pullover: 2 (3, 3, 3) skeins of Vanilla (100) for A; 1 skein each of Pistachio (169) for B, Sugar Plum (144) for C, and Mint (156) for D. For Blankee: 2 skeins of Vanilla (100) for A, and 1 skein each of Pistachio (169) for B, Sugar Plum (144) for C, and Mint (156) for D
Size 7 (4.5 mm) knitting needles or size needed to obtain gauge
Six, JHB International buttons, Bubbles (36671), size ⅝"; yarn needle

GAUGE:

In St st with larger needles, 17 sts and 24 rows = 4"/10 cm. TAKE TIME TO CHECK YOUR GAUGE.

STITCHES USED:

Gum Balls (a multiple of 4 sts + 3 sts; a rep of 18 rows)
Row 1 (RS): With B, knit.
Row 2: With B, purl.
Rows 3–4: Rep Rows 1-2.
Row 5: With A, k3; * drop next st off needle and unravel 4 rows down; insert left needle from front into color A st in 5th row below and knit it, catching the 4 loose strands into the st; k3; rep from * across.
Row 6: With A, purl.
Rows 7–10: With C, rep Rows 1–4.
Row 11: With A, k1; rep from * of Row 5, ending last rep k1 instead of k3.
Row 12: With A, purl.
Rows 13–16: With D, rep Rows 1–4.
Row 17: Rep Row 5.
Row 18: Rep Row 6.
Rows 19–22: With B, rep Rows 1–4.
Rows 23–24: With A, rep Rows 11–12.
Rows 25–28: With C, rep Rows 1–4.
Rows 29–30: With A, rep Rows 5–6.
Rows 31–34: With D, rep Rows 1–4.
Rows 35–36: With A, rep Rows 11–12.
For Pullover, Rows 1–18 are worked once. For Blankee, rep R5ows 1–36 for pattern.

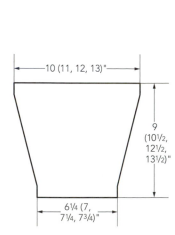

INSTRUCTIONS:
PULLOVER BACK

Beg at lower edge with A, cast on 55 (63, 67, 71) sts. Knit 9 rows for Garter St Border. Purl across next row. Work Rows 1–18 of Gum Balls. Beg St st (knit RS rows, purl WS rows). Work even to approx 12 (14, 15, 17)" from beg, ending with a RS row. Knit 9 rows.

Neck Shaping

K 20 (23, 24, 25) sts, join a new ball of yarn and bind off center 15 (17, 19, 21) sts, k to end. Working sides separately and at the same time, k 9 more rows. Bind off rem sts for each shoulder.

FRONT

Work as for Back to approx 10 (12, 13, 15)" from beg, ending with a RS row.

Neck Shaping

Row 1 (WS): P20 (23, 24, 25), k15 (17, 19, 21), p to end.
Row 2 and each following RS row: Knit.
Row 3: P19 (22, 23, 24), k17 (19, 21, 23), p to end.
Row 5: P18 (21, 22, 23), k19 (21, 23, 25), p to end.
Row 7: P17 (20, 21, 22), k21 (23, 25, 27), p to end.

Row 9: P16 (19, 20, 21), k23 (25, 27, 29), p to end.
Row 10: K20 (23, 24, 25) sts, bind off center 15 (17, 19, 21) sts, k to end. Place first 20 (23, 24, 25) sts onto a holder.

Right Shoulder

Row 1 (WS): P 16 (19, 20, 21), k4.
Row 2: Knit.
Rows 3–10: Rep Rows 1-2.
Rows 11–15: Knit all sts.
Row 16: K3; [yo, k2tog, k 4 (5, 5, 6)] sts twice yo, k2tog, k 3 (4, 5, 4)—3 buttonholes.
Rows 17–19: Knit. Bind off.

Left Shoulder

With WS facing; join A to rem sts, k4, p to end. **Row 2:** Knit. **Row 3:** K4, p to end. **Rows 4–9:** Rep Rows 2-3. **Row 10:** Knit. **Rows 11–15:** Knit all sts. **Row 16:** K 3 (4, 5, 4); [yo, k2tog, k4 (5, 5, 6)] twice; yo, k2tog, k3—3 buttonholes. **Rows 17–19:** Knit. Bind off.

140

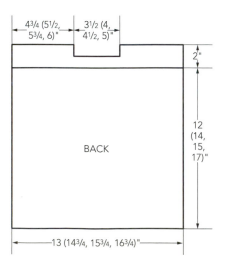

4¾ (5½, 5¾, 6)" | 3½ (4, 4½, 5)"

2"

BACK

12 (14, 15, 17)"

13 (14¾, 15¾, 16¾)"

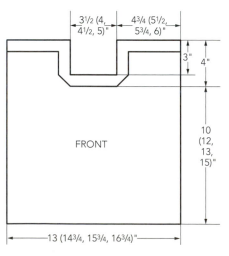

3½ (4, 4½, 5)" | 4¾ (5½, 5¾, 6)"

3"
4"

FRONT

10 (12, 13, 15)"

13 (14¾, 15¾, 16¾)"

10 (11, 12, 13)"

9 (10½, 12½, 13½)"

6¼ (7, 7¼, 7¾)"

SLEEVES (make two)

With A, cast on 27 (29, 31, 33) sts. Knit 9 rows for Garter St Border. Purl next row. Inc 1 st each edge every 4th row 3 (2, 0, 0) times and every 6th row 5 (7, 10, 11) times. Work even on 43 (47, 51, 55) sts to approx 9 (10½, 12½, 13½)" from beg, ending with a WS row. Bind off.

FINISHING

Overlap front over back for 1" at shoulders and sew armhole edges in place. Place markers 5¼ (5¾, 6¼, 6¾)" each side of shoulder seams. Set in sleeves between markers. Join underarm and side seams. Sew buttons opposite buttonholes.

Bubble Gum Bobbles (make one each of B, C, and D) Leaving 6" tails at each end, cast on 2 sts. Inc in each st— 4 sts. P 1 row, k 1 row, p 1 row. Slip next st with yarn at back, k3tog, pass slipped st over k3tog. Fasten off. Tie tails tog in a square knot. Center first Bubble Gum at center and just beneath neckband. Take tails to WS and tie in an overhand knot. Trim ends. Place rem two Bubble Gum on either side of first.

BLANKEE (measures approx 24×28")

Note: The Blankee is worked using 2 colors in most rows. When changing color, bring new strand from under present strand for a "twist" to prevent holes. Use separate strands of yarn for each color section. Cut and join as necessary.

With A, cast on 101 sts. Knit 9 rows for Garter St Border. Purl next row.
Body Pattern, Row 1 (RS): K5-A, with B knit across, k5-A. **Row 2:** K5-A, with B purl across, ending k5A. Pattern is now set. Keeping 5 sts each edge in Garter St with A, cont in Gum Ball pattern until piece measures approx 27" from beg, ending with Row 6, 12, or 18. With A, knit 10 rows. Bind off. Weave in loose ends along WS of fabric.

totally-tied jacket

photos on pages 118–119

SKILL LEVEL: Easy

SIZES: 4 (SIX, 8, 10)
Note: The pattern is written for the smallest size with changes for larger sizes in parentheses. When only one number is given, it applies to all sizes. For ease in working, before you begin, circle the numbers pertaining to the size you are knitting.

FINISHED MEASUREMENTS:
Chest (tied): 29¼ (31, 33¾, 36½)"
Length: 14 (15½, 17½, 18½)"

MATERIALS:
Patons, Decor, 75% acrylic/25% wool, worsted-weight yarn (210 yards per ball): 3 (4, 4, 5) balls of Winter White (1614)
Size 7 (4.5 mm) knitting needles or size needed to obtain gauge
Sizes 6 (4 mm) knitting needles
Yarn needle

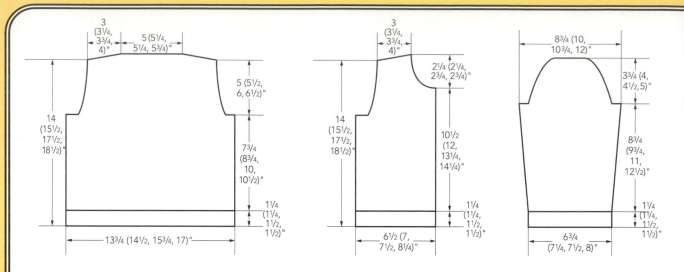

GAUGE:

In St st (knit RS rows, purl WS rows) with larger needles, 20 sts and 26 rows = 4"/10 cm. TAKE TIME TO CHECK YOUR GAUGE.

SPECIAL ABBREVIATIONS:

Ssk: Slip next 2 sts knitwise, one at a time to right-hand needle, insert tip of left-hand needle into fronts of these 2 sts and k them tog.

P2tog-b: Turn work slightly, insert needle from left to right into back loops of 2nd and first sts, p these two sts tog.

STITCHES USED:

Seed St (worked over an odd number of sts)
Row 1 (RS): * K1, p1; rep from * to last st, k1.
Row 1 forms Seed St Pat.

INSTRUCTIONS:
BACK

Beg at lower edge with smaller needles, cast on 67 (71, 77, 83) sts.
Work Seed St for 8 (8, 10, 10) rows, inc 2 sts evenly across last row—69 (73, 79, 85) sts.
Change to larger needles and work in St st until work from beg measures approx 9 (10, 11½, 12)", ending with a WS row.

Armhole Shaping

At the beg of the next 2 rows, bind off 3 (3, 4, 4) sts— 63 (67, 71, 77) sts.
Dec 1 st each end of needle on NEXT and following alt rows until there are 55 (59, 63, 69) sts. Cont even until back measures approx 14 (15½, 17½, 18½)" from beg, ending with a WS row.

Shoulder Shaping

Bind off 7 (8, 9, 10) sts beg next 2 rows, then 8 (8, 9, 10) sts beg following 2 rows.
Bind off rem 25 (27, 27, 29) sts.

LEFT FRONT

Beg at lower edge with smaller needles, cast on 31 (33, 37, 39) sts.
Work Seed St for 8 (8, 10, 10) rows, inc 2 (2, 1, 2) st(s) evenly across last row—33 (35, 38, 41) sts. Change to larger needles and work in St st until work from beg measures approx 9 (10, 11½, 12)", ending with a WS row.

Armhole Shaping

At the beg of the next row, bind off 3 (3, 4, 4) sts—30 (32, 34, 37) sts. Work 1 row even.
Dec 1 st at beg of NEXT and following alt rows until there are 26 (28, 30, 33) sts. Cont even until piece measures approx 11¾ (13¼, 14¾, 15¾)" from beg, ending with a RS row.

Neck Shaping

Bind off 5 (6, 6, 7) sts, purl to end of row. Dec 1 st at neck edge on next 5 (5, 3, 3) rows, then on following alt row(s) 1 (1, 3, 3) time(s)—15 (16, 18, 20) sts. Cont even until piece measures same length as Back, ending with a WS row.

Shoulder Shaping

Bind off 7 (8, 9, 10) sts beg next row. Work 1 row even. Bind off rem 8 (8, 9, 10) sts.

RIGHT FRONT

Work as for Left Front, reversing all shapings.

SLEEVES (make two)

Beg at lower edge with smaller needles, cast on 33 (35, 35, 37) sts.
Work Seed St for 8 (8, 10, 10) rows, inc 1 (1, 3, 3) st(s) evenly across last row—34 (36, 38, 40) sts.
Change to larger needles and work 8 rows in St st, beg with a RS row.

142

Shape sides by inc 1 st each edge on NEXT and every 8th (6th, 6th, 6th) row 2 (3, 2, 6) times, then on 10th (8th, 8th, 8th) rows 2 (3, 5, 3) times—44 (50, 54, 60) sts. Work even until Sleeve measures approx 10 (11, 12½, 14)" from beg, ending with a WS row.

Sleeve Cap Shaping
Bind off 3 (3, 4, 4) sts beg next 2 rows—38 (44, 46, 52) sts. Dec 1 st each end of needle on NEXT and following alt rows until there are 22 (28, 30, 30) sts, then on every row until there are 10 (12, 12, 14) sts. Bind off rem sts.

FINISHING

Right Front Edging: With RS facing and smaller needles, pick up and knit 57 (63, 65, 75)
sts evenly across front edge between cast on edge and neck edge.
Work 7 (7, 9, 9) rows in Seed St , placing a marker at neck edge on 4th (4th, 6th, 6th) row.
Next Row (make ties) (RS):
Bind off 16 (18, 20, 22) sts; pat across next 5
sts (including st on needle after bind off); turn. Leave rem sts on a spare needle.
Cont in pat on these 5 sts until Tie measures approx 7½". Bind off in pat.
Rejoin yarn to rem sts; bind off next 13 (15, 15, 19) sts; pat across next 5 sts (including st on needle after bind off); turn. Leave rem sts on a spare needle.
Cont in pat on these 5 sts until Tie measures approx 7½". Bind off in pat.
Rejoin yarn to rem sts; bind off next 13 (15, 15, 19) sts;

pat across last 5 sts (including st on needle after bind off).
Cont in pat on these 5 sts until Tie measures approx 7½". Bind off in pat.
Left Front Edging: With RS facing and smaller needles, pick up and knit 57 (63, 65, 75) sts evenly across front edge between neck edge and cast-on edge.
Work 7 (7, 9, 9) rows in Seed St, placing a marker at neck edge on 4th (4th, 6th, 6th) row.
Next Row (make ties) (RS):
Pat across first 5 sts; turn. Leave rem sts on a spare needle. Cont in pat on these 5 sts until Tie measures approx 7½". Bind off in pat.
* Rejoin yarn to rem sts; bind off next 13 (15, 15, 19) sts; pat across next 5 sts (including st on needle after bind off); turn. Leave rem sts on a spare needle.
Cont in pat on these 5 sts until Tie measures approx 7½". Bind off in pat.* Rep from * to * once more.
Rejoin yarn to rem sts; bind off last 16 (18, 20, 22) sts.
Sew shoulder, side and sleeve seams. Set in sleeves.
Pocket: With smaller needles, cast on 9 sts. Work 1 row in Seed St.
Inc 1 st each end of next and following alt rows until there are 15 sts, taking inc sts into Seed St Pat.
Cont in Seed St Pat until Pocket measures approx 3". Bind off in pat. Sew to Left Front approx 5 (5½, 6, 6)" down from shoulder seam and 2½ (2¾, 3, 3¼)" in from front edge.
Collar: With smaller needles, cast on 85 (87, 87, 91) sts. Work 2 rows in Seed St.

Row 3: Pat 27 (27, 27, 29) sts, (p1, k1, p1) all in next st, pat 29 (31, 31, 31) sts, (p1, k1, p1) all in next st, pat 27 (27, 27, 29) sts—89 (91, 91, 95) sts.
Rows 4–6: Work even in pat.
Row 7: K1, k2tog, pat 25 (25, 25, 27) sts, (k1, p1, k1) all in next st, pat 31 (33, 33, 33) sts, (k1, p1, k1) all in next st, pat 25 (25, 25, 27) sts, ssk, k1—91 (93, 93, 97) sts.
Row 8: K2, pat to last 2 sts, k2.
Row 9: K1, p2tog, pat to last 3 sts, p2tog-b, k1—89 (91, 91, 95) sts.
Row 10: Work even in pat.
Row 11: K1, k2tog, pat 22 (22, 22, 24) sts, (p1, k1, p1) all in next st, pat 33 (35, 35, 35) sts, (p1, k1, p1) all in next st, pat 22 (22, 22, 24) sts, ssk, k1—87 (89, 89, 93) sts.
Row 12: As Row 8.
Row 13: As Row 9—85 (87, 87, 91) sts.
Row 14: Work even in pat.
Row 15: K1, k2tog, pat to last 3 sts, ssk, k1—83 (85, 85, 89) sts.
Bind off in pat. Sew cast-on edge of Collar to neck edge between markers.

ballerina-neck sweater

photos on pages 120–121

SKILL LEVEL: Easy

SIZES: XS (S, MEDIUM, L, XL)
Note: The pattern is written for the smallest size with changes for larger sizes in parentheses. When only one number is given, it applies to all sizes. For ease in working, before you begin, circle the numbers pertaining to the size you are knitting.

FINISHED MEASUREMENTS:
Bust: 34 (36, 38, 40, 42)"
Length: 21 (21½, 21½, 22, 22½)"

MATERIALS:
Classic Elite, Star, 99% cotton/1% lycra, sport-weight yarn (112 yards per skein): 9 (10, 11, 12, 13) skeins of Pink (5132)
Size 7 (4.5 mm) knitting needles or size needed to obtain gauge
Size 6 (4 mm) knitting needles
2 stitch holders
Yarn needle

GAUGE:
In St st (knit RS rows, purl WS rows) with larger needles, 22 sts and 30 rows = 4"/10 cm.
TAKE TIME TO CHECK YOUR GAUGE.

SPECIAL ABBREVIATIONS:
M1: Lift running thread before next stitch onto left-hand needle and knit in its back loop to make one stitch.
Ssk: Slip next 2 sts knitwise, one at a time to right-hand needle, insert tip of left-hand needle into front of these 2 sts and k them tog.
P1-b: Turn work slightly, insert right-hand needle into stitch from left to right and purl.
P2tog-b: Turn work slightly, insert right-hand needle into second and then first sts from left to right; purl the 2 sts tog.

**INSTRUCTIONS
BACK**
** Beg at lower edge with larger needles cast on 92 (96, 104, 108, 112) sts.
Row 1 (RS): K2tog; * (yo) twice, ssk, k2tog; rep from * to last 2 sts, (yo) twice, ssk.

Row 2: P1; * p1 into first yo, then p1-b into next yo, p2; rep from * to last 3 sts; p1 into first yo, then p1-b into next yo, p1. Rep last 2 rows for openwork ribbing until work measures approx 5½" ending with Row 2.
Next Row (RS): Knit, dec 9 (7, 9, 7, 7) sts evenly across row—83 (89, 95, 101, 105) sts. Beg with a purl row, work 3 more rows St st.
Side Shaping
Inc Row (RS): K2, M1; k to last 2 sts, M1, k2.
Work 7 rows even.
Rep last 8 rows 4 times more —93 (99, 105, 111, 115) sts. Cont even until work from beg measures approx 13½" ending with a purl row.
Armhole Shaping
Bind off 6 (7, 8, 9, 10) sts beg next 2 rows—81 (85, 89, 93, 95) sts.
Next Row: K2, k2tog, k to last 4 sts, ssk, k2.
Work 1 row even.
Rep last 2 rows 5 (6, 6, 8, 8) times more—69 (71, 75, 75, 77) sts. **
Cont even until piece

measures approx 19¾ (20¼, 20¼, 20¾, 21¼)" from beg, ending with a purl row.

Neck Shaping and Shoulder Shaping

For First Shoulder: K17 (17, 19, 19, 19) (neck edge); turn, leave rem sts on a spare needle.

Dec 1 st at neck edge on next 6 rows—11 (11, 13, 13, 13) sts. Work 1 row even. Bind off 5 (5, 6, 6, 6) sts beg next row. Work 1 row even. Bind off rem 6 (6, 7, 7, 7) sts. For Second Shoulder: With RS of work facing, slip next 35 (37, 37, 37, 39) sts onto a st holder. Join yarn to rem sts and work to correspond to First Shoulder, reversing all shapings.

FRONT

Work from ** to ** as for Back. Cont even until piece measures approx 18½ (19, 19, 19½, 20)" from beg, ending with a purl row.

Neck and Shoulder Shaping

For First Shoulder: K19 (19, 21, 21, 21) (neck edge); turn, leave rem sts on a spare needle.

Dec 1 st at neck edge on next 4 rows, then on following alt rows 4 times— 11 (11, 13, 13, 13) sts. Cont even until piece measures same length as Back to beg of shoulder shaping, ending with a purl row. Bind off 5 (5, 6, 6, 6) sts beg next row. Work 1 row even. Bind off rem 6 (6, 7, 7, 7) sts. With RS of work facing, slip next 31 (33, 33, 33, 35) sts onto a st holder. Join yarn to rem sts and work to correspond to First Shoulder, reversing all shapings.

SLEEVES (make two)

With larger needles cast on 60 (60, 64, 64, 64) sts. Work 4" in openwork ribbing as given for Back, ending with Row 2.

Next Row (RS): K2tog; * yo, ssk, k2tog; rep from * to last 2 sts, yo, ssk—45 (45, 48, 48, 48) sts.
Beg with a purl row, cont in St st for 5 rows.

Side Shaping

Inc Row (RS): K2, M1, k to last 2 sts, M1, k2.
Work 5 rows even.
Rep last 6 rows 12 (14, 13, 14, 15) times more—71 (75, 76, 78, 80) sts.
Cont even until sleeve measures approx 18½" from beg, ending with a purl row.

Sleeve Cap Shaping

Bind off 3 (3, 4, 4, 5) sts beg next 2 rows—65 (69, 68, 70, 70) sts.
Next Row: K2, k2tog, k to last 4 sts, ssk, k2.
Work 1 row even.
Rep last 2 rows 11 (14, 15, 17, 20) times more—41 (39, 36, 32, 28) sts.
Next Row: K2, k2tog, k to last 4 sts, ssk, k2.

145

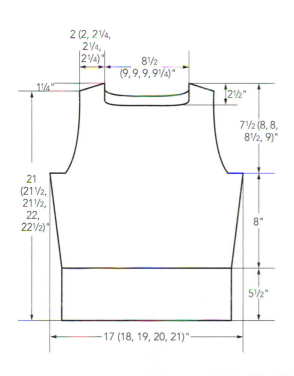

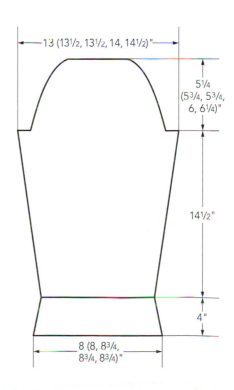

Next Row: P2, p2tog-b, p to last 4 sts, p2tog, p2.
Rep last 2 rows 6 (5, 4, 3, 1) time(s) more. Bind off rem 13 (15, 16, 18, 20) sts.

FINISHING
Sew right shoulder seam.
Neck Edging: With RS facing and smaller needles, pick up and knit 18 sts down right front neck edge. K31 (33, 33, 33, 35) from front st holder. Pick up and knit 18 sts up right front neck edge and 7 sts down right back neck edge. K35 (37, 37, 37, 39) from back st holder. Pick up and knit 7 sts up left back neck edge—116 (120, 120, 120, 124) sts.
Knit 2 rows. Bind off knitwise (WS).
Sew left shoulder and neck edging seam. Set in sleeves. Sew side and sleeve seams.

off to brunch

photos on pages 122–123

SKILL LEVEL: Intermediate

SIZES: XS (S, MEDIUM, L, XL)
Note: The pattern is written for the smallest size with changes for larger sizes in parentheses. When only one number is given, it applies to all sizes. For ease in working, before you begin, circle the numbers pertaining to the size you are knitting.

FINISHED MEASUREMENTS:
Bust: 36 (40½, 44, 48½, 52)"
Length: 24 (24¼, 25, 25¼, 25¾)"

MATERIALS:
Muench Yarns, G118 Via Mala, 100% merino wool, bulky-weight yarn (74 yards per skein): 11 (13, 15, 16, 18) skeins of Silver (17) for A and 1 (1, 1, 2, 2) skein(s) of White (5) for B.
Size 10 (6.00 mm) knitting needles or size needed to obtain gauge
20"-length circular needles; Size 9 (5.5 mm), Size 10 (6 mm), and
Size 10½ (6.5 mm)
2 ring-type stitch markers
3 stitch holders
Yarn needle

GAUGE:
In Easy Ribs Pattern with middle-size needles, 14 sts and 24 rows = 4"/10 cm.
TAKE TIME TO CHECK YOUR GAUGE.

SPECIAL ABBREVIATIONS:
Ssk: Slip next 2 sts knitwise, one at a time to right-hand needle, insert tip of left-hand needle into fronts of these 2 sts and k them tog.
M1: Lift running thread before next stitch onto left-hand needle and knit in its back loop to make one stitch.
Pm: Place marker.

STITCHES USED:
Easy Ribs (a multiple of 2 sts + 1 st; a rep of 2 rows)
Row 1 (WS): P1; (k1, p1) across.
Row 2: Knit.
Rep Rows 1–2 for Easy Ribs.

Center Panel (over 19 sts; a rep of 16 rows)
Row 1 (RS): K4; (p1, k4) 3 times.
Row 2: P3, k2, p3, k1, p1, k1, p3, k2, p3.
Row 3: K2, p1, k1, p1, k2, (p1, k1) twice, p1, k2, p1, k1, p1, k2.
Row 4: P1, k1, p1, k2, (p1, k1) 4 times, p1, k2, p1, k1, p1.

Row 5: (P1, k1) twice, p2, (k1, p1) 3 times, k1, p2, (k1, p1) twice.
Row 6: P1, k1, p1, k2, (p1, k1) 4 times, p1, k2, p1, k1, p1.
Row 7: K2, p1, k1, p1, k2, (p1, k1) twice, p1, k2, p1, k1, p1, k2.
Row 8: P3, k2, p3, k1, p1, k1, p3, k2, p3.
Row 9: K4; (p1, k4) 3 times.
Row 10: P3, k2, p9, k2, p3.
Row 11: K2, p1, k1, p1, k4, p1, k4, p1, k1, p1, k2.
Row 12: P1, k1, p1, k2, p3, k1, p1, k1, p3, k2, p1, k1, p1.
Row 13: (P1, k1) twice, p1, k2, (p1, k1) twice, p1, k2, (p1, k1) twice, p1.
Row 14: P1, k1, p1, k2, p3, k1, p1, k1, p3, k2, p1, k1, p1.
Row 15: K2, p1, k1, p1, k4, p1, k4, p1, k1, p1, k2.
Row 16: P3, k2, p9, k2, p3.
Rep Rows 1–16 for Center Panel.

Note: Borders on lower edges of each piece are added after the knitting is completed.

INSTRUCTIONS:
BACK
Beg at lower edge, above border, with middle-size needles and A, cast on 63 (71, 77, 85, 91) sts. Work Easy Ribs to approx 16" from beg, ending with a WS row.
Raglan Shaping
Bind off 2 sts at beg of next 2 rows—59 (67, 73, 81, 87) sts.
Dec Row 1 (RS): K1, ssk, k across, ending k2tog, k1.
Row 2: P2, pattern across, ending p2. Rep last 2 rows for 8 (15, 17, 24, 27) times more. **Next Dec Row** (SIZES XS, S, M, L ONLY): K1, ssk, k across, ending k2tog, k1.
Row 2: P2, pattern across, ending p2. **Row 3:** Knit. **Row 4:** As Row 2. Rep last 4 rows for 6 (3, 3, 0, 0) times more. ALL SIZES: When piece measures approx 24 (24¼, 25, 25¼, 25¾)" from beg, ending with a WS row, place rem 27 (27, 29, 29, 31) sts onto holder.

FRONT
* Beg at lower edge, above border, with middle-size needles and A, cast on 29 (33, 36, 40, 43) sts. With a 2nd ball, rep from * for second side. Work sides separately and at the same time as follows:
Row 1 (WS): (P1, k1) 11 (13, 14, 16, 18) times, p0 (0, 1, 1, 0), pm, p7. Second Side: P7, pm, p0 (0, 1, 1, 0), (k1, p1) 11 (13, 14, 16, 18) times.
Row 2: K22 (26, 29, 33, 36), (p1, k1) twice, p1, k2. Next Side: K2, (p1, k1) twice, p1, k22 (26, 29, 33, 36).
Row 3: (P1, k1) 11 (13, 14, 16, 18) times, p0 (0, 1, 1, 0), p1, k1, p1, k2, p2. Second Side: P2, k2, p1, k1, p1, p0 (0, 1, 1, 0), (k1, p1) for 11 (13, 14, 16, 18) times.
Row 4: K to marker, k2, p1, k1, p1, k2. Next Side: K2, p1, k1, p1, k2, k to end.
Row 5: (P1, k1) for 11 (13, 14, 16, 18) times, p0 (0, 1, 1, 0), p3, k2, p2. Cast on 5 sts for Center Front, then with same strand work Second Side as follows: p2, k2, p3, p0 (0, 1, 1, 0), (k1, p1) 11 (13, 14, 16, 18) times—63 (71, 77, 85, 91) sts.
Upper-Body Pattern
Keeping 22 (26, 29, 33, 36) sts on outside edges in Easy Rib pattern as est, work Center Panel beg with Row 1 across center 19 sts. Pattern is now set. Cont as est to approx 16" from beg, ending with a WS row.
Raglan Shaping
As for Back. AT THE SAME TIME, when piece measures approx 20 (20¼, 21, 21¼, 21¾)" from beg, place markers on each side of center 9 (9, 11, 11, 13) sts and end with a WS row.

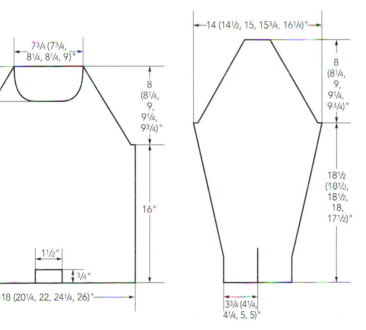

7¾ (7¾, 8¼, 8¼, 9)"

4"

8 (8¼, 9, 9¼, 9¾)"

24 (24¼, 25, 25¼, 25¾)"

16"

1½"

¾"

18 (20¼, 22, 24¼, 26)"

14 (14½, 15, 15¾, 16¼)"

8 (8¼, 9, 9¼, 9¾)"

18½ (18½, 18½, 18, 17½)"

3¾ (4¼, 4¼, 5, 5)"

Neck Shaping

Work est pattern across to marker; join a new ball of yarn and bind off center 9 (9, 11, 11, 13) sts; work est pattern to end of row. Working sides separately and at the same time, bind off 3 sts at each neck edge once, 2 sts each neck edge once, and 1 st each neck edge once. Cont even to same length as Back. On next RS row for each side, k3tog and fasten off.

SLEEVES (make two)

* Beg at lower edge, above border, with middle-size needles and A, cast on 13 (15, 15, 17, 17) sts. With a 2nd ball, rep from * for second side. Working sides separately and at the same time, work Easy Ribs to approx 3" from beg, ending with a WS row. Joining Row: K12 (14, 14, 16, 16) sts, k2tog, k to end; leaving a tail, cut 2nd ball of yarn, k across—25 (29, 29, 33, 33) sts.
Inc Row 1 (RS): K1, M1, k across, ending M1, k1. Including new sts into Easy Ribs as they accumulate, inc 1 st each edge every 6th row 4 (1, 4, 1, 6) time(s) more and every 8th row 7 (9, 7, 9, 5) times. Work even on 49 (51, 53, 55, 57) sts to approx 18½ (18½, 18½, 18, 17½)" from beg, ending with a WS row.
Raglan Shaping
Bind off 2 sts at beg of next 2 rows—45 (47, 49, 51, 53) sts.
Dec Row 1 (RS): K1, ssk, k across, ending k2tog, k1.
Row 2: P2, pattern across, ending p2. Rep last 2 rows 12 (13, 13, 14, 15) times more, then dec every 4th row 5 (5, 6, 6, 6) times. When piece measures approx 26½ (26¾, 27½, 27¼, 27¼)" from beg, end with a WS row. Place rem 9 sts onto a holder.

FINISHING

Join raglan sleeves to front and back.

Collar

With RS facing, using smallest circular needle and A, k across 27 (27, 29, 29, 31) sts for back neck, k 9 sleeve sts, pick up and k 22 sts evenly spaced along side of neck, pick up and k 9 (9, 11, 11, 13) sts at front neck and 22 sts along side of neck, k 9 sts from sleeve—98 (98, 102, 102, 106) sts. Place a marker to indicate beg of rnd. Work (k1, p1) rib around for 6 times. Change to middle-size circular needle and rib around for 7 rnds. Change to largest circular needle and rib 9 rnds. Change to B, purl 1 rnd, knit 1 rnd, purl 1 rnd. Bind off loosely and knitwise on WS of fabric.

Sleeve Edging

With RS facing using middle-size needles and B, pick up and k 1 st in each cast-on st along edge, pick up and k 14 sts along each side of vent, pick up and k 1 st in each cast on st along next edge. Knit 2 rows. Bind off knitwise and loosely on WS of fabric.

Back Edging

With RS facing using middle-size circular needle and B, pick up and k 1 st in each cast-on st along edge. Knit 2 rows. Bind off knitwise and loosely on WS of fabric.

Front Edging

As for Back Edging, except, pick up and k 13 sts around center shaping. Complete as est.
Join underarm and side seams.

so-soft baby sweater, bonnet, and booties

photos on pages 124–125

SKILL LEVEL: Easy

SIZES: Infants 3 (SIX, 9, 12) months.
Note: The pattern is written for the smallest size with changes for larger sizes in parentheses. When only one number is given, it applies to all sizes. For ease in working, before you begin, circle the numbers pertaining to the size you are crocheting.

FINISHED MEASUREMENTS:
Chest (buttoned): 20 (22, 24, 26)"
Length: 9½ (11, 12¼, 13¼)"

MATERIALS:
Coats & Clark, J&P Coats LusterSheen, 100% acrylic, sport-weight yarn
(150 yards per ball): 3 (4, 4, 5) balls of Crystal Pink (206) for Cardigan, plus 2 balls for Bonnet and Booties
Size 3/D (3.25 mm) aluminum crochet hook or size needed to obtain gauge
Tapestry needle
Four ⅜-inch buttons

GAUGE:
In Body Pattern, 23 sts and 16 rows = 4"/10 cm.
TAKE TIME TO CHECK YOUR GAUGE.

SPECIAL ABBREVIATIONS:
Sc2tog: Draw up a lp in each of next 2 sts, yo and draw through all 3 lps on hook.

STITCHES USED:

Body Pattern (a multiple of 2 sts + 1 st; a rep of 2 rows)

Row 1 (RS): Ch 1, hdc in first sc; * ch 1, sk 1 sc, hdc in next sc; rep from * across; turn.

Row 2: Ch 1, sc in hdc; * sc in ch-1 sp, sc in hdc; rep from * across; turn.

Rep Rows 1–2 for Body Pattern.

INSTRUCTIONS:

BACK

Beg at the lower edge, ch 64 (70, 76, 82).

Foundation, Row 1 (RS): Hdc in 2nd ch from hook; (ch 1, sk 1 ch, hdc in next ch) across; turn. Counting each ch-1 sp as a stitch—63 (69, 75, 81) sts.

Row 2: Ch 1, sc in each hdc and ch-1 sp across; turn. Work in Body Pattern to approx 5 (6, 7, 7¾)" from beg ending with a RS row. Fasten off.

Armhole Shaping

With WS facing, join yarn with a sl st in 7th st from right edge. Ch 1, sc in same hdc as joining. Sc in each of next 50 (56, 62, 68) sts, leaving rem 6 sts unworked; turn. Cont est pat on rem 51 (57, 63, 69) sts to approx 9 (10½, 11¾, 12¾)" from beg ending with a RS row. Fasten off.

RIGHT FRONT

Beg at the lower edge, ch 30 (32, 36, 38). Rep Foundation Rows 1–2 as for Back—29 (31, 35, 37) sts. Work in Body Pattern to approx 5 (6, 7, 7¾)" from beg ending with a RS row. Fasten off.

Armhole Shaping

With WS facing, join yarn with a sl st in 7th st from right edge. Ch 1, sc in same hdc as joining. Sc in each of next 22 (24, 28, 30) sts; turn. Cont est pat on rem 23 (25, 29, 31) sts to approx 5½ (6½, 7¾, 8¾)" from beg ending with a RS row.

Neck Shaping

Row 1 (WS): Ch 1, sc in each hdc and ch-1 sp across ending sk last hdc; turn.

Row 2: Ch 1, sk first sc, hdc in next sc; (ch 1, sk 1 sc, hdc in next sc) across; turn. Rep Rows 1–2 until 11 (13, 15, 17) sts rem. Cont in pat to same length as Back ending with a WS row. Fasten off.

LEFT FRONT

Work as for Right Front to approx 5 (6, 7, 7¾)" from beg ending with a RS row.

Armhole Shaping

Work Body Pattern, Row 2 across leaving last 6 sts unworked—23 (25, 29, 31) sts; turn. Cont in pat to approx 5½ (6½, 7¾, 8¾)" from beg ending with a RS row.

Neck Shaping

Row 1 (WS): Ch 1, sk first hdc; (sc in ch-1 sp, sc in hdc) across; turn.

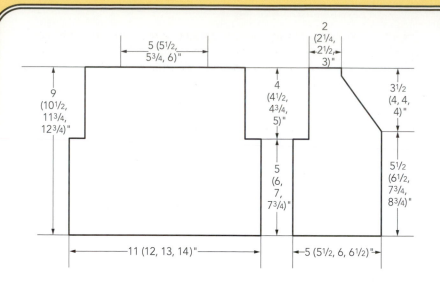

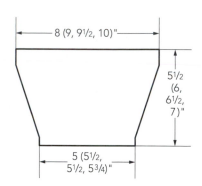

Row 2: Ch 1; (hdc in sc, ch 1, sk 1 sc) across ending hdc in sc, sk last sc; turn.
Rep Rows 1–2 until 11 (13, 15, 17) sts rem. Cont in pat to same length as Back ending with a WS row. Fasten off.

SLEEVES (make two)
Beg at the lower edge, ch 30 (32, 32, 33). Rep Foundation Rows 1–2 as for Back—29 (31, 31, 33) sts.
Sleeve Shaping
Inc Row 1 (RS): Ch 1, in first sc (hdc, ch 1, hdc); * ch 1, sk 1 sc, hdc in next sc; rep from * across to last 2 sc, ch 1, sk 1 sc, in last sc (hdc, ch 1, hdc)—4 sts added; turn.
Row 2: Rep Row 2 of Body Pattern across; turn.
Rep Rows 1–2 for Body Pattern 1 (2, 3, 2) times more; then inc each edge (as before) every 4th row 2 (2, 2, 3) times—45 (51, 55, 57) sts. Cont in pat without increasing to approx 5½ (6, 6½, 7)" from beg ending with a WS row. Fasten off.

FINISHING
Join shoulder seams. Sewing skipped underarm sts to sides of sleeves for square

armholes, set in sleeves. Join underarm and side seams.
Front Band
With RS facing, join yarn with a sl st in lower corner of right front. Ch 1, work 24 (29, 34, 37) sc evenly spaced to V-neck shaping, 3 sc in corner. Work 17 (19, 19, 19) sc evenly spaced along neck edge to shoulder. For back neck; sc2tog, sc in each of next 25 (27, 29, 31) sc, sc2tog. Work 17 (19, 19, 19) sc evenly spaced along neck edge, 3 sc in corner, 24 (29, 34, 37) sc evenly spaced to lower edge; turn.
Row 2: Ch 1, sc in 44 (51, 56, 59) sc, sc2tog, sc in 23 (25, 27, 29) sc, sc2tog; sc in each rem sc to end; turn.
Row 3: Ch 1, sc in first 2 (4, 6, 6) sc; * ch 1, sk 1 sc, sc in each of next 6 (7, 8, 9) sc; rep from * twice more. Ch 1, sk 1 sc, sc in next sc, 3 sc in next sc for corner, sc in each sc around dec 1 st at each back neck edge and working 3 sc in opposite corner; turn.
Row 4: Ch 1, sc in each sc and ch-1 sp around, dec 1 st at each back neck edge. Fasten off.

Body Edging
With RS facing beg in a ch-1 sp at lower edge and near a seam, join yarn, ch 3, sl st in same sp. * Sl st in hdc, in next ch-1 sp (sl st, ch 3, sl st); rep from * to band. Working along band and then body, * sl st in sc, in next sc (sl st, ch 3, sl st) around. Cont est pattern around to beg. Fasten off.
Sleeve Edgings: Work as for Body Edging.
Sew buttons opposite buttonholes.

BONNET
[approx 13 (13¾, 14½, 15)" across widest portion]
Beg at the back, ch 60 (64, 68, 72). Rep Foundation Rows 1–2 as for Back—59 (63, 67, 71) sts.
Note: Ties on baby bonnets can be dangerous. Never leave a bonnet on a baby when she is alone.
Shaping
Row 1 (RS): Ch 1, in first sc (hdc, ch 1, hdc); (ch 1, sk 1 sc, hdc in next sc) across ending (hdc, ch 1, hdc) in last sc—4 sts added; turn.

Row 2: Ch 1, sc in each hdc and ch-1 sp across; turn. Rep Rows 1–2 for 3 times more—75 (79, 83, 87) sts. Work Body Pattern to approx 4¼ (4¾, 5¼, 5¾)" from beg ending with Row 2. Work 6 sc rows. Fasten off.

Trim

With RS facing, join yarn with a sl st in ch-1 sp at right edge of back; ch 3, sl st in same sp as joining. (Sl st, ch 3, sl st) in each ch-1 sp across. * (Sl st, ch 3, sl st) over hdc post, sk sc post; rep from * along side **. Working in front lps only, [(sl st, ch 3, sl st) in lp, sk next lp] across brim. Rep from * to ** for second side. At end, fasten off. With WS facing and working in rem lps along brim [(sl st, ch 3, sl st) in lp, sk next lp] across and fasten off.

Ties

For back tie; ch 150. Sl st in 2nd ch from hook and in each ch across. Fasten off. Weave tie through Foundation Row 1; tie into a bow. Pull tie ends to softly gather opening; tie into a bow. For first side tie; ch 300 and complete as for back tie. For second side tie; ch 250 and complete as for back tie. Fold first tie in half and weave through last eyelet row before the sc band. Fold second tie in half and join with a sl st through the loop formed by the fold on the first tie. Position ties so that there is an equal amount on each side. Tie ends into overhand knots.

BOOTIES [approx 3 (3¼, 3½, 3¾)" long]

Ch 14 (15, 16, 17).

Rnd 1: 2 dc in 4th ch from hook. Dc in each of next 9 (10, 11, 12) ch, 5 dc in last ch for toe. Working along opposite edge, dc in each of next 9 (10, 11, 12) ch, 2 dc in last ch. Join with a sl st 3rd ch of beg ch-3.

Rnd 2: Ch 3 (counts as dc), dc in same dc as join. 2 dc in each of next 2 dc, dc in each of next 9 (10, 11, 12) dc. For toe; 2 dc in next 2 dc, 3 dc in next dc, 2 dc in next 2 dc. Dc in each of next 9 (10, 11, 12) dc, 2 dc in each of next 2 dc—39 (41, 43, 45) sts.

Rnd 3: (Ch 1, sl st) in front lp of each dc around for rick rack edging.

Rnd 4: Ch 1, sl st in first rem back lp. Ch 1, hdc in same lp as join. Hdc in next 2 lps, sc in each rem lp around to last 3 lps, hdc in last 3 lps—39 (41, 43, 45) sts. Join with a sl st in first hdc.

Rnd 5: Ch 1, hdc in same hdc as joining and in next hdc, sc in each of next 11 (12, 13, 14) sts, sc2tog, hdc in next 10 sts, sc2tog, sc in each of next 11 (12, 13, 14) sts, hdc in last st; join.

Rnd 6: Ch 1, hdc in first 2 hdc, sc in each of next 11 (12, 13, 14) sts, sc2tog, hdc in next 8 sts, sc2tog, sc in each of next 11 (12, 13, 14) sts, hdc in last st; join.

Rnd 7: Ch 1, hdc in first 2 hdc, sc in each of next 11 (12, 13, 14) sts, sc2tog, hdc in next 6 sts, sc2tog, sc in each of next 11 (12, 13, 14) sts, hdc in last st; join.

Rnd 8: Ch 1, hdc in first 2 hdc, sc in each of next 11 (12, 13, 14) sts, sc2tog, hdc in next 4 sts, sc2tog, sc in each of next 11 (12, 13, 14) sts, hdc in last st; join.

Rnd 9: Ch 1, hdc in first 2 hdc, sc in each of next 11 (12, 13, 14) sts, sc2tog, hdc in next 2 sts, sc2tog, sc in each of next 11 (12, 13, 14) sts, hdc in last st—29 (31, 33, 35) sts. Sl st in front lp of first hdc to join.

Rnd 10: Working in front lps (ch 3, sl st in same lp); * sk next lp, in next lp (sl st, ch 3, sl st); rep from * around ending, sl st in same lp as first sl st.

Rnd 11: Sl st in first rem back lp. Ch 1, hdc in same lp as sl st. (Ch 1, sk 1 lp, hdc in next lp) around ending ch 1, sl st in first hdc.

Rnd 12: Ch 1, sc in each hdc and ch-1 sp around; sl st in front lp of first sc.

Rnd 13: Rep Rnd 10.

Rnd 14: Sl st in each rem back lp around. Fasten off. Tie; ch 100. Sl st in 2nd ch from hook and in each ch across. Fasten off. Weave through ch-1 spaces at top of bootie. Tie ends into an overhand knot.

151

weekends up north

photos on pages 126–127

SKILL LEVEL: Intermediate

SIZES: S (MEDIUM, L, XL)
Note: The pattern is written for the smallest size with changes for larger sizes in parentheses. When only one number is given, it applies to all sizes. For ease in working, before you begin, circle all numbers pertaining to the size you are knitting.

FINISHED MEASUREMENTS:
Bust: 42 (44, 46, 48)"
Length: 27½"

MATERIALS:
Brown Sheep, Lamb's Pride Bulky, 85% wool/15% mohair, bulky-weight yarn (125 yards per skein): 9 (9, 10, 10) skeins of Khaki (M-18)
Size 10½ (6.5 mm) knitting needles or size needed to obtain gauge
Yarn needle

GAUGE:
In textured-pattern stitches, 13 sts and 18 rows = 4"/10cm. TAKE TIME TO CHECK YOUR GAUGE.

152

SPECIAL ABBREVIATIONS:
MB: In next st (k1, yo) 3 times, k1 = 7 sts made. Slip 2nd, 3rd, 4th, 5th, and 6th stitches over first stitch one at a time.

STITCHES USED:
Pattern A (15 sts for each panel; a rep of 14 rows)
Row 1 and each following WS Row: P15.
Row 2: K15.
Row 4: K6, p3, k6.
Row 6: K5, p5, k5.
Row 8: K4, p3, k1, p3, k4.
Row 10: K3, p3, k3, p3, k3.
Row 12: K2, p3, k5, p3, k2.
Row 14: K15.
Rep Rows 1–14 for Pattern A.

Pattern B (a multiple of 9 sts + 3 sts; over 7 rows)
Row 1 (WS): Knit.
Row 2: Knit.

Row 3: * P4, k4, p1; rep from * across, ending p4 rather than p1.
Row 4: * K3, p1, k4, p1; rep from * across, ending k3.
Row 5: * K3, p6; rep from * across, ending k3.
Row 6: Knit.
Row 7: Knit.
Rows 1–7 complete Pattern B.

Pattern C (7 sts for each panel; a rep of 14 rows)
Row 1 (RS): K7.
Row 2: P7.
Rows 3–4: Rep Rows 1–2.
Row 5: K3, MB, k3.
Row 6: P7.
Row 7: K7.
Rows 8–9: Rep Rows 6-7.
Row 10: P3, k1, p3.
Row 11: K2, p1, k1, p1, k2.
Row 12: P1, k1, p3, k1, p1.
Row 13: Rep Row 11.
Row 14: Rep Row 10.
Rep Rows 1–14 for Pattern C.

INSTRUCTIONS:
BACK
Beg at lower edge, cast on 69 (72, 75, 78) sts. Knit 5 rows for Garter St Border.
Set Up for Body Pattern as follows (WS): K3; * Row 1 of Pattern A over 15 sts, k1 (2, 3, 4); rep from * twice more, Row 1 of Pattern A over 15 sts, k3.

Row 2: K3; * Row 2 of Pattern A over 15 sts, k1 (2, 3, 4); rep from * twice more, Row 2 of Pattern A over 15 sts, k3. Pattern is now set. Rep pattern rows as est until piece measures approx 16½" from beg, ending with Row 14.

For Pattern B: Work first 2 rows.
Row 3: K3, p3 (0, 1, 3); pattern Row 3 across, ending p3 (0, 2, 3), k3.
Row 4: K6 (3, 5, 6); pattern Row 4 across, ending k 6 (3, 4, 6).
Row 5: K3, p3 (0, 1, 3); pattern Row 5 across, ending p3 (0, 2, 3), k3.
Rows 6–7: Work last 2 rows of Pattern B.

For Pattern C: Row 1 (RS): Knit.
Row 2: K3; * [p7, k1 (1, 1, 2)] 3 times, p7 *, k1 (4, 7, 4); rep from * to * once more, k3.
Rows 3–4: As Rows 1–2.
Row 5: K3; * [k3, MB, k3, k1 (1, 1, 2)] 3 times, k3, MB, k3 *, k1 (4, 7, 4); rep from * to * once more, k3.

Row 6: As Row 2.
Row 7: Knit.
Rows 8–9: As Row 6–7.
Row 10: K3; * [p3, k1, p3, k1 (1, 1, 2)] 3 times, p3, k1, p3 *, k1 (4, 7, 4); rep from * to * once more, k3.
Row 11: K3; * [k2, p1, k1, p1, k2, k1 (1, 1, 2)] 3 times, k2, p1, k1, p1, k2 *, k1 (4, 7, 4); rep from * to * once more, k3.
Row 12: K3; * [p1, k1, p3, k1, p1, k1 (1, 1, 2)] 3 times, p1, k1, p3, k1, p1*, k1 (4, 7, 4); rep from * to * once more, k3.
Row 13: As Row 11.
Row 14: As Row 10.
Pattern is now set. Cont as est until piece measures approx 27½" from beg, ending with a WS row.
Shoulder and Neck Shaping
Bind off 12 (12, 13, 13) sts each shoulder edge once and 12 (13, 13, 14) sts each shoulder edge once. Bind off rem 21 (22, 23, 24) sts.

FRONT
Work as for Back until piece measures approx 26½" from beg, ending with a WS row.
Neck Shaping
Pattern across first 31 (32, 33, 34) sts, join a 2nd ball of yarn and bind off center 7 (8, 9, 10) sts, work to end of row. Working sides separately and at the same time, at each neck edge bind off 3 sts once, 2 sts once, and 1 st twice. Cont even on rem 24 (25, 26, 27) sts for each shoulder to same length as Back, ending with a WS row.
Shoulder Shaping
Work as for Back.

SLEEVES (make two)
Beg at lower edge, cast on 31 (32, 33, 34) sts. Knit 5 rows for Garter St Border.
Set Up for Pattern A, Row 1 (WS): P15, k1 (2, 3, 4), p15. For remainder of sleeve, center 31 (32, 33, 34) sts will be worked in Pattern A over first and last 15 sts with center 1 (2, 3, 4) sts in Garter St.

Working new sts in Garter St, inc 1 st each edge every 6th row 0 (0, 2, 6) times, every 8th row 6 (6, 7, 4) times, and every 10th row 2 (2, 0, 0) times. Cont in pattern on 47 (48, 51, 54) sts to approx 17" from beg, ending with a WS row. Bind off.

FINISHING
Join left shoulder seam.
Neckband
With RS facing, pick up and k21 (22, 23, 24) sts evenly spaced along back neck, 11 sts along side of neck, 7 (8, 9, 10) sts along front neck and 11 sts along side of neck—50 (52, 54, 56) sts. Knit 2 rows. Purl 1 row. Knit 1 row. **Row 5 (WS):** P5 (6, 7, 8); (k4, p5) across, ending k4, p5 (6, 7, 8). **Row 6:** K0 (1, 2, 3), p1; (k3, p1, k4, p1) across, ending k3, p1, k0 (1, 2, 3). **Row 7:** P1 (2, 3, 4); (k3, p6) across, ending k3, p1 (2, 3, 4). **Row 8:** Knit. **Row 9:** Purl. **Row 10:** Knit. Bind off loosely and knitwise.
Join right shoulder and neckband seam.
Place markers 7 (7½, 8, 8½)" each side of shoulder seams. Set in sleeves between markers. Join underarm and side seams, leaving last 5" free along each side for vents.

153

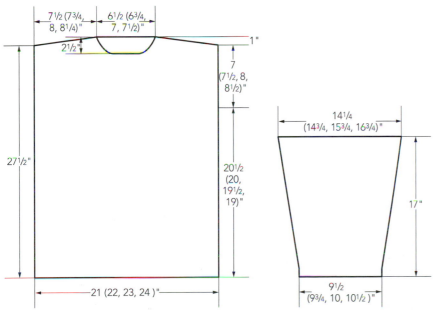

it's the

Accessorize your wardrobe with hand-knit and crocheted accents that show off your talent and creativity. Quick to make and so much fun to use, this chapter's collection includes playful tote bags, scarves, mittens, socks, shawls, pillows, hats, exercise mats, and tank tops. Even first-time knit and crochet enthusiasts can complete these nifty projects with ease.

little things

KNOCKOUT SOCKS

Warm your toes with striped tube socks knit in fun and fancy colors. They stay put with comfy banded cuffs. Instructions are on page 173.

kicked back

SO-SIMPLE HATS AND MITTENS
The wintry season is much more enjoyable
when you wear colorful hats and mittens
to keep you warm. Instructions
for these hats and mittens and other color
choices begin on page 174.

warm

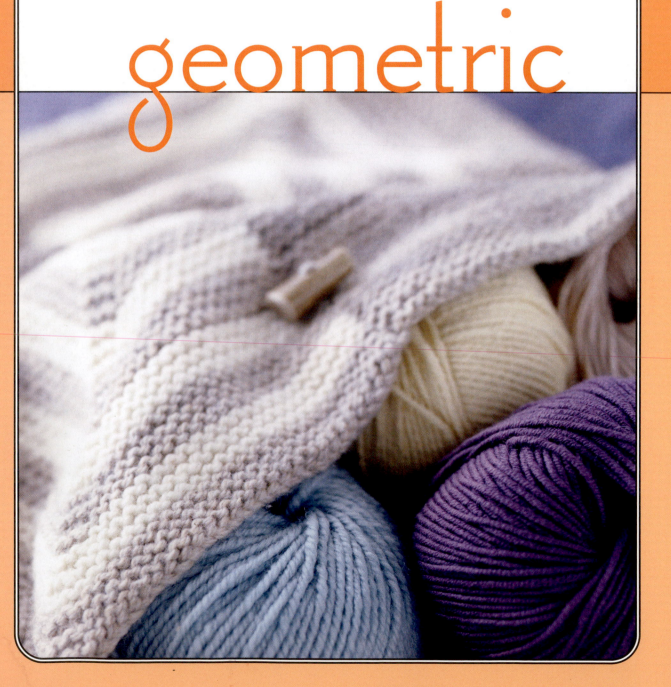

GRAPHIC BAG

*Knit eight striped panels to create this
sophisticated square tote bag.
The strap and sides are one piece, making
construction a breeze. Instructions
begin on page 175.*

geometric

GLITTER SHAWL

Blend two metallic gold yarns
to make this easy-to-knit project
and wrap your shoulders in a chic
shiny shawl for your next
dressy occasion. Instructions
begin on page 176.

elegant

textured

CHA-CHA SCARF

This vibrant crocheted fuzzy scarf is long enough to
wear over your head when you're caught without a hat.
The ends are finished with long fluffy fringes.
Instructions begin on page 177.

STYLIN' CROCHETED SET

For a hip youthful look, this shawl, belt, and hat are bright and breezy. Crocheted with a I/9 hook, this open pattern tops off an outfit with contemporary style. Instructions begin on page 178.

exotic

tasseled

SHOWY CROCHETED SCARF

Wine-color yarn is the basis for this plush crocheted scarf. Easy enough for a beginner, the scarf has pointed ends and generous tassels.

Instructions begin on page 179.

SQUARES-ON-SQUARES PILLOW

Three contrasting hues make this stripes-on-checks
pillow stunning. This pillow is created in the
same fashion as the tote bag on pages 160–161.
Instructions for the pillow are on page 180.

graphic

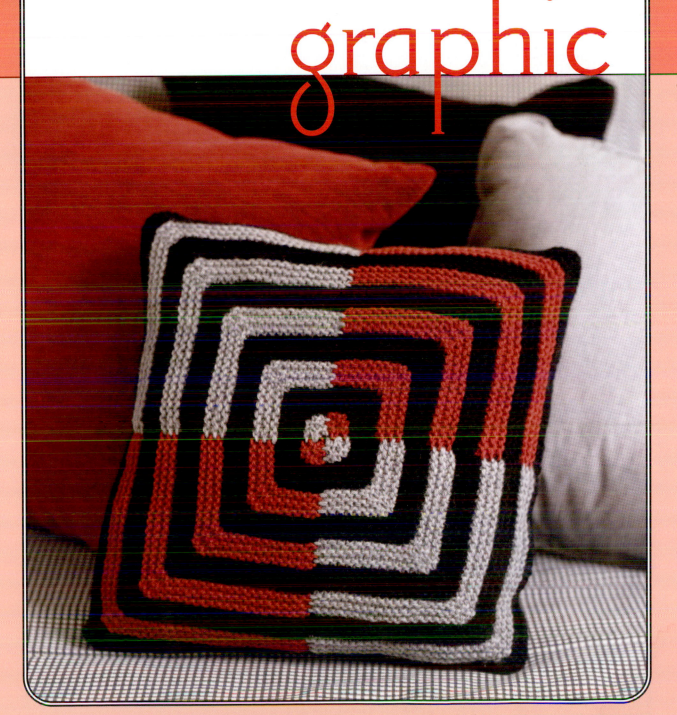

relaxed

STRIPED BAG
AND EXERCISE MAT

Give your exercise or yoga workout a boost with a matching mat and bag knit in two tones of green. The mat is worked solely in garter stitches, that also embellish the bag rim and straps. Instructions begin on page 180.

EASY CROCHET HAT AND BAG

Dotted with splashes of color and bobble details, this cotton crocheted combo is pure fun. Once you learn the bobble stitch, you'll want to add these playful touches to your sweaters too! Instructions begin on page 182.

171

fun

cool

SUMMER TOP

This easy-to-knit cotton top works up so quickly, you'll want one in every color. The garter-stitch accents create raised borders on the neckline and hem. Instructions begin on page 183.

knockout socks

photos on pages 156–157

SKILL LEVEL: Easy

SIZE: Child's 4–6 (8–10 or average woman)

FINISHED SIZES:
Circumference: 6¾ (7½, 8)"
Length: 11¾ (13½, 15)"

MATERIALS:
Patons, Look at Me, 60% acrylic/40% nylon, sport-weight yarn (152 yards per skein): For Solid Color Socks: 2 skeins of Fun 'n Games (6377) or Bright Lilac (6383). For Striped Socks: 1 skein each of Peacock (6370) for MC and Green Apple (6362) for A
Size 5 (3.75 mm) set of four double pointed knitting needles (dpn) or size needed to obtain gauge
Yarn needle

GAUGE:
In St st (knit every rnd), 24 sts and 32 rnds = 4"/10 cm. TAKE TIME TO CHECK YOUR GAUGE.

INSTRUCTIONS:
SOLID SOCKS
(make two alike)
Cast on 40 (44, 48) sts. Divide sts evenly on 3 needles. Join in rnd, placing a marker on first st. Work 2 (2, 2½)" in (k2, p2) ribbing.
Knit in rnds until work from beg measures approx 10½ (12, 13½)".
Size 8 to 10 only: Next Rnd: (K9, k2tog) 4 times—40 sts. Knit 1 rnd even.
Toe Shaping (all sizes)
Rnd 1: (K6, k2tog) 5 (5, 6) times—35 (35, 42) sts.
Rnd 2 and all alt rnds: Knit.

Rnd 3: (K5, k2tog) 5 (5, 6) times—30 (30, 36) sts.
Rnd 5: (K4, k2tog) 5 (5, 6) times—25 (25, 30) sts.
Cont in this manner, dec 5 (5, 6) sts evenly around every alt rnd until there are 10 (10, 12) sts. Break yarn, leaving a long end. Draw end tightly through rem sts. Weave in ends.

STRIPED SOCKS
(make two alike)
Stripe Pattern
Rnds 1–5: With A, knit.
Rnds 6–10: With MC, knit.
These 10 rnds form Stripe Pat.

With MC, cast on 40 (44, 48) sts. Divide sts evenly on 3 needles. Join in rnd, placing a marker on first st. Work 2 (2, 2½)" in (k2, p2) ribbing.
Cont in Stripe Pat and work as given for Solid Socks.

so-simple mittens

photos on pages 158–159, this page, and opposite

SKILL LEVEL: Easy

SIZES: SMALL (M, L)

FINISHED MEASUREMENTS:
Width: 4 (4½, 5)"
Length: 9½ (10¼, 11)"

MATERIALS:
Patons Shetland Chunky,
   75% acrylic/25% wool, bulky
   weight yarn (148 yards per
   ball): For all sizes, 1 ball of
   Zircon (3734) OR Plum Crazy
   (3728) OR Mango (3714)
Size 6 (4 mm) knitting
   needles or size needed to
   obtain gauge
Yarn needle
Two ring-type stitch markers

GAUGE:
In St st (knit RS rows, purl
WS rows), 15 sts and 24 rows
= 4"/10 cm.
TAKE TIME TO CHECK
YOUR GAUGE.

SPECIAL ABBREVIATIONS:
M1: Lift running thread
before next stitch onto left-
hand needle and knit in its
back loop to make one stitch.
Ssk: Slip next 2 sts knitwise,
one at a time to right-hand
needle, insert tip of left-hand
needle into fronts of these 2
sts and k tog.
Pm: Place a marker.

INSTRUCTIONS:
FIRST MITTEN
Cast on 25 (29, 33) sts. Beg
with a purl row, work 5 St st
rows. Inc 1 st each edge now
and then every 4th row twice
more—31 (35, 39) sts. Work
even to approx 2½ (3, 3½)"
from beg, ending with a
WS row.

Thumb
Row 1 (RS): K15 (17, 19) sts,
pm, M1, k1, M1, pm, k15
(17, 19).
Row 2: Purl.
Row 3: K to marker, sl
marker, M1, k to marker, M1,
sl marker, k to end of row.
Rep Rows 2-3 until there are
13 (13, 15) sts between
markers. Purl next row,
removing markers. Next
Row: K across, placing thumb
sts onto a spare strand of
yarn. Work even on the 30
(34, 38) sts until piece
measures approx 8½ (9, 9½)"
from beg, ending with a WS
row and pm after 15th (17th,
19th) st.

Top Shaping
Dec Row (RS): Ssk, k to 2 sts
before marker, k2tog, sl
marker, ssk, k to last 2 sts,
k2tog. Next Row: Purl. Rep
last 2 rows until 18 (18, 22)
sts rem. On next RS row,
(k2tog) across. P9 (9, 10).
Leaving a long tail for
sewing, cut yarn.

Closure
Thread tail into yarn needle.
Beg with the last st on needle,
take yarn back through rem
sts, twice. Pull up to tightly
close opening. Join sides tog.

Thumb
With RS facing, return sts to
needle. Join yarn and k13
(13, 15). Next Row: P5 (5, 7),

p2tog, p6. Work 6 (6, 8) more St st rows on the 12 (12, 14) sts. Next Row: (K2tog) across. Cut yarn, leaving a 10" tail. Rep Closure as for Top. Join thumb seam. Darn opening. Weave in loose ends on WS of fabric.

SECOND MITTEN
Work as for First Mitten.

so-simple hats

photos on pages 158–159, this page, and opposite

SKILL LEVEL: Easy

SIZE: To fit an average adult

FINISHED SIZE: 19" around

MATERIALS:
Patons, Shetland Chunky, 75% acrylic/25% wool, chunky-weight yarn (148 yards per skein): 1 skein of Mango (03714), or Plum Crazy (03728), or Zircon (03734)

Size 10 (6 mm) knitting needles or size needed to obtain gauge
Yarn needle

GAUGE:
In St st (knit RS rows, purl WS rows, 15 sts and 20 rows = 4"/10 cm.
TAKE TIME TO CHECK YOUR GAUGE.

SPECIAL ABBREVIATIONS:
M1: Lift running thread before next stitch onto left-hand needle and knit in its back loop to make one stitch.

Note: Add a pom-pom to top of cap if desired.

INSTRUCTIONS:
Cast on 67 sts. Work 4 rows Garter St (knit every row) noting first row is WS.
Next Row (WS): (K13, M1) 4 times, k15—71 sts.
Beg with a knit row, work in St st until Cap measures approx 4¾" from beg, ending with a purl row.

Top Shaping
Row 1 (RS): K1; * k2tog, k8; rep from * to end of row— 64 sts.
Row 2 and all WS rows: Purl.
Row 3: K1; * k2tog, k7; rep from * to end of row—57 sts.
Row 5: K1; * k2tog, k6; rep from * to end of row—50 sts.
Cont in this manner, dec 7 sts evenly across RS rows until there are 8 sts. Break yarn, leaving a long end. Draw end through rem sts and fasten securely. Sew center back seam. Weave in ends.

graphic bag

photos on pages 160–161

SKILL LEVEL: Easy

SIZE: Approx 12½" square.

MATERIALS:
Patons, Classic Merino Wool, 100% wool, worsted-weight yarn (223 yards per ball): 2 balls of Natural Mix (229) for MC; 1 ball each of Dark Natural Mix (228) for A, and Aran (202) for B
Size 7 (4.5 mm) knitting needles or size needed to obtain gauge.
1" toggle
Tapestry needle
Six safety pins for markers

GAUGE:
In Garter St (knit every row), 18½ sts and 38 rows = 4"/10 cm.
TAKE TIME TO CHECK YOUR GAUGE.

Rep from * to * 3 times more
—8 sts.
Change to A.
Next Row: K2, (k2tog, ssk) over center 4 sts, k2.
Next Row: Knit.
Next Row: K1, (k2tog, ssk) over center 4 sts, k1.
Next Row: Knit.
Next Row: K2tog, ssk—2 sts.
Next Row: K2tog; fasten off.

MOTIF 2 (make 4)
Work as Motif 1 substituting B for A.

FINISHING
Sew Motifs together as shown for Front and Back.

Strap and Sides: With MC, cast on 10 sts. For Sides: Work in Garter St for 37½", placing a set of markers on each side as follows: First set of markers 12½" from cast on edge, second set of markers 12½" from first set and third set of markers 12½" from second set of markers. **For Strap:** Cont in Garter St until work from third set of markers measures approx 31"—piece should measure approx 68½". Bind off. Sew Front and Back of bag to Sides placing cast on edge at top right corner of Bag and placing markers at corners. Sew end of Strap to cast on edge. Sew toggle centered onto Front, 2" from opening. Make a twisted cord using 3 strands of MC, 8" long. Holding strands tog, tie an overhand knot at one end; twist tightly. Tie a second overhand knot 4½" from first. Trim away excess. Sew ends of cord together at center Back to form loop. Weave in ends.

glitter shawl

photos on pages 162–163

SKILL LEVEL: Easy

SPECIAL ABBREVIATIONS:
Ssk: Slip next 2 sts knitwise, one at a time to right-hand needle, insert tip of left-hand needle into fronts of these 2 sts and k them together.

Note: Carry yarn loosely up side of work when not in use.

INSTRUCTIONS
MOTIF 1 (make 4)
With MC, cast on 60 sts.
Row 1 (WS): Knit.
Row 2: K28, (k2tog, ssk) over center 4 sts, k28.
Row 3: Knit.
Row 4: Knit to center 4 sts, (k2tog, ssk) over center 4 sts, knit to end.
Row 5: Knit.
* Change to A.
Next 6 rows: Rep Rows 4 and 5 for 3 times.
Change to MC.
Next 6 rows: Rep Rows 4 and 5 for 3 times.*

FINISHED MEASUREMENT:
Approx 40" wide × 23" deep.

MATERIALS:
Berroco, Metallic FX, 85% rayon/15% metallic, worsted-weight yarn (85 yards per skein): 5 skeins of Gold (1001) for MC

Berroco, Mirror FX, 100% polyester, novelty-weight yarn (60 yards per skein): 6 skeins of Gold/White (9001) for A

Size 9 (5.5 mm) knitting needles or size needed to obtain gauge

Yarn needle

GAUGE:
In Pattern using 1 strand each of MC and A , 15 sts and 22 rows = 4"/10 cm.
TAKE TIME TO CHECK YOUR GAUGE.

SPECIAL ABBREVIATIONS:
K-inc: Knit in front and back of next stitch.

INSTRUCTIONS:
Beg at point, with 1 strand each of MC and A, cast on 3 sts.

Row 1 (WS): K3.

Row 2: K-inc in first st, k-inc in next st, k1—5 sts.

Row 3: K.

Row 4: K-inc in first st, k to last 2 sts, k-inc in next st, k1.

Row 5: K, wrapping yarn twice around needle for each st.

Row 6: K, dropping extra loops.

Rows 7–8: Rep Row 4.

Rep Rows 5 to 8 until there are 143 sts.

Bind off loosely.

cha-cha scarf

photos on pages 164–165

SKILL LEVEL: Easy

SIZE: 5 × 50"

MATERIALS:
Patons, Grace, 100% cotton, sport-weight yarn (136 yards per ball): 1 ball of Fuchsia (60438) for MC

Patons, Cha Cha, 100% nylon, novelty weight yarn (77 yards per ball): 1 ball of Be Bop (02003) for color A

Size 6/G (4 mm) crochet hook or size needed to obtain gauge

GAUGE:
In Body Pattern, 16 sts and 8 rows = 4"/10 cm.
TAKE TIME TO CHECK YOUR GAUGE.

Note: To change color, make a dc until 2 lps rem on hook, with next color yo and complete the dc.

INSTRUCTIONS:
With MC, ch 197.

Row 1 (RS): Dc in 5th ch from hook (counts as dc, ch-1, dc). * Ch 1, sk next ch, dc in next ch; rep from * across, ending change to A in last st—195 sts; turn.

Row 2: With A, ch 3 (counts as dc); * dc in next ch-1 sp, ch 1; rep from * across, ending dc in last ch-1 sp, dc in last dc, and change to MC in last st; turn.

Row 3: With MC, ch 4 (counts as dc, ch-1), skip next dc; * dc in next ch-1 sp, ch 1; rep from * across, ending sk 1 dc, dc in last dc; turn.

Row 4: Using MC, rep Row 2. Do not change color.

Row 5: With MC, rep Row 3 and change to A in last st. For Body Pattern, rep Rows 2–5 again, then rep Rows 2-3 once more. Fasten off.

Fringe

With RS facing, join A with sl st in right corner of short side of scarf, ch 1, sc in same sp as joining. * Ch 42, sc around dc post of next row; rep from * across. Fasten off. Work opposite end as est.

stylin' crocheted set

photos on pages 166–167

SKILL LEVEL: Easy

SIZE: The three garments will fit an average-size adult.

FINISHED MEASUREMENTS:
Belt: 3 × 38", excluding fringe
Cap: 19" around
Shawl: 45" wide × 20" deep excluding fringe

MATERIALS:
Patons, Katrina, 92% rayon/8% polyester, worsted-weight yarn (163 yards per ball): Ocean (10120); 1 ball for Belt, 1 ball for Cap and 3 balls for Hip Shawl
Size I/9 (5.5 mm) crochet hook or size needed to obtain gauge

GAUGE:
5 arches and 7 rows = 4"/10 cm.
TAKE TIME TO CHECK YOUR GAUGE.

INSTRUCTIONS:
BELT
Ch 11. **Foundation Row:** Sc in 2nd ch from hook; (ch 4, sk 2 ch, sc in next ch) 3 times—3 arches; turn.
Row 1: Ch 5 (counts as dc + ch-2), sc in first ch-4 arch; (ch 4, sc in next ch-4 arch) twice, ch 2, dc in last sc; turn.
Row 2: Ch 1, sc in first dc; (ch 4, sc in next ch-4 arch) twice, ch 4, sc in 3rd ch of beg ch-5; turn.
Rep Rows 1–2 until work when slightly stretched measures approx 38". Fasten off.
Fringe
Cut 2 strands of yarn measuring approx 27" each. Holding strands tog, fold in half to form a loop, take loop through arch at end of belt. Add two fringe to each arch along each end of belt. Trim evenly.

CAP
Ch 57; being careful to keep ch untwisted, join with sl st to form a ring.
Rnd 1: Ch 1, sc in same ch as joining, sc in each ch around; join with sl st in first sc—57 sts.
Rnd 2: Ch 1, sc in same sc as joining, sc in each sc around; join.
Rnd 3: Ch 1, sc in same sc as joining; (ch 4, sk 2 sc, sc in next sc) around to last 2 sc, sk 2 sc, dc in first sc—19 arches.
Rnd 4: Ch 1, sc in top of last dc; * ch 4, sc in next ch-4 arch; rep from * around, ending ch 2, dc in first sc.
Rnds 5–12: As Rnd 4.
Rnd 13: Ch 1, sc in top of last dc; * ch 3, sc in next ch-4 arch; rep from * around, ending ch 1, dc in first sc—19 ch-3 sps.
Rnd 14: Ch 1, sc in top of last dc; * ch 3, sc in next ch-3 sp; rep from * around, ending ch 1, dc in first sc.
Rnd 15: Ch 1, sc in top of last dc; * ch 2, sc in next ch-3 sp; rep from * around, ending ch 1, hdc in first sc—19 ch-2 sps.
Rnd 16: Ch 1, sc in top of last hdc; * ch 4, sk next ch-2 sp, sc in next ch-2 sp; rep from * around, ending ch 2, dc in first sc—10 ch-4 arches.
Rnd 17: Ch 1, sc in top of last dc; * ch 4, sc in next ch-4 arch; rep from * around, ending ch 2, dc in first sc.
Rnd 18: Ch 1, sc in top of last dc; * ch 3, sc in next ch-4 arch; rep from * around, ending ch 1, dc in first sc.
Rnd 19: Ch 1, sc in top of last dc; * ch 3, sc in next ch-3 sp; rep from * around,

ending ch 1, dc in first sc—
10 ch-3 spaces.
Rnd 20: Ch 2; * yo and draw
up a lp in next ch-3 sp, yo
and draw through 2 lps on
hook; rep from * around,
ending yo and draw through
all 10 lps on hook. Fasten off.

SHAWL
Ch 170. **Foundation Row
(RS):** Sc in 2nd ch from hook
and in each ch across—169
sc; turn.
Row 1: Ch 1, sc in first sc;
* ch 4, sk 2 sc, sc in next sc;
rep from * across to last 3 sts,
ch 1, sk 2 sc, dc in last sc—
56 arches; turn.
Row 2: Ch 3 (counts as ch-3
sp), sk ch-1 sp, sc in first ch-4
arch; * ch 4, sc in next ch-4
arch; rep from * across,
ending ch 1, dc in last ch-4
arch; turn.
Row 3: Ch 3 (counts as ch-3
sp), sk ch-1 sp, sc in first ch-4
arch; * ch 4, sc in next ch-4
arch; rep from * across, ending
ch 1, dc in ch-3 sp; turn.
Rep Row 3 until the following
row has been completed: Ch
3, sc in first ch-4 arch, ch 1,
dc in ch-3 sp; turn.
Last Row: Ch 3, sc in ch-3 sp.
Fasten off.
Fringe
Cut two strands of yarn
measuring approx 14" long.
Holding strands tog, fold in
half to form loop, take
loop through a sp along
the diagonal edge of
shawl; take ends
through loop and pull up
to tighten. Add a fringe
to each sp along the two
diagonal edges of the shawl.
Trim evenly.

showy crocheted scarf

photo on page 168

SKILL LEVEL: Easy

SIZE: Approx 8 × 64",
excluding tassels

MATERIALS:
Coats & Clark, Red Heart
Plush, 80% acrylic/20%
nylon, worsted-weight yarn
(6 ounces per skein): 1 skein
of Wine (9782)
Size I/9 (5.5 mm) crochet
hook or size needed to
obtain gauge

GAUGE:
In pattern, 15 sts and 12 rows
= 4"/10 cm.
TAKE TIME TO CHECK YOUR
GAUGE.

SPECIAL ABBREVIATIONS:
Sc2tog: Draw up a loop in each
of next 2 stitches, yo and draw
through all 3 loops on hook.
Sc3tog: Draw up a loop in each
of next 3 stitches, yo and draw
through all 4 loops on hook.

INSTRUCTIONS:
Beg at lower edge and above
the border, ch 30.

Foundation Row: Sc in
second ch from hook; (ch 1,
sk 1 ch, sc in next ch) across
—29 sts counting each ch-1
as a stitch; turn.
Row 1 (WS): Ch 1, sc in first
sc, sc in ch-1 sp; (ch 1, sk 1
sc, sc in next ch-1 sp) across,
ending sc in last sc; turn.
Row 2: Ch 1, sc in first sc; (ch
1, sk 1 sc, sc in next ch-1 sp)
across, ending ch 1, sk 1 sc,
sc in last sc; turn.
Rep Rows 1–2 for pattern
until piece measures approx
54" from beg, ending with a
RS row.

First Border
Dec Row: Ch 1, sc2tog over
first sc and ch-1 sp, pattern
across, ending sc2tog over
ch-1 sp and last sc.
Rep Dec Row until 5 sts rem.
Next Row: Ch 1, sc2tog, ch 1,
sc2tog—3 sts; turn. Next
Row: Ch 1, sc in first sc, in
ch-1 sp (yo and draw up a
loop) 5 times, yo and draw
through 10 loops on hook,
yo and draw through 2 loops
on hook, sc in last sc; turn.
Next Row: Ch 1, sc3tog.
Fasten off.

Second Border
With the WS facing, join yarn
with sl st in first sc of
Foundation Row. Work as for
First Border.

Tassel (make two)
Cut 24 strands measuring approx 10" each. Hold strands in a bundle and fold in half to form a loop. Take a separate strand through fold and tie securely at top. Wrap another strand 3 times, tightly ½" from first tie and secure in place. With top tie, join to end of Border. Trim ends.

squares-on-squares pillow

photos on page 169

SKILL LEVEL: Easy

SIZE: To fit a 14" square pillow form.

MATERIALS:
Patons, Classic Merino Wool, 100% wool, worsted-weight yarn (223 yards per ball): 1 ball each of Black (226) for MC and Rich Red (207) for A, and Grey Mix (224) for B
Size 7 (4.5 mm) knitting needles or size needed to obtain gauge
14"-square pillow form
Tapestry needle

GAUGE:
In Garter St (knit every row), 18½ sts and 38 rows = 4"/10 cm.
TAKE TIME TO CHECK YOUR GAUGE.

SPECIAL ABBREVIATIONS:
Ssk: Slip next 2 sts knitwise, one at a time to right-hand needle, insert tip of left-hand needle into fronts of these 2 sts and k them together.

Note: Carry yarn loosely up side of work when not in use.

INSTRUCTIONS:
See GRAPHIC BAG INSTRUCTIONS beginning on *page 175*. For the pillow, work 4 each of Motif 1 and Motif 2. For each side of pillow top, sew 4 motifs together as shown in photo, *above*. Sew pillow tops together along 3 sides. Insert pillow form and sew remaining side closed.

striped bag and exercise mat

photo on page 170

MAT

SKILL LEVEL: Beginner

SIZE: 20 × 30"

MATERIALS:
Elmore-Pisgah, Peaches & Créme, 100% cotton, double-worsted yarn (400 yards per cone): 1 cone each of Verde Green (53) for color A and Apple Green (51) for color B
Size 10½ (6.5 mm) knitting needles or size needed to obtain gauge
Yarn needle

GAUGE:
In Garter Stitch (knit every row), 12 stitches and 24 rows (or 12 ridges) = 4"/10 cm.

TAKE TIME TO CHECK YOUR GAUGE.

Note: Cut and join yarn as necessary, leaving 6" tails to weave in later. When working the center of the mat (2 rows A, 2 rows B) carry yarn not in use loosely along side edge.

INSTRUCTIONS:

With color A, cast on 60 sts. Noting that first row is RS, knit 20 rows = 10 ridges. Change to color B and knit 2 rows = 1 ridge. Knit 16 rows with A. Knit 2 rows with B. Knit 12 rows with A. Knit 2 rows with B. Knit 8 rows with A. Knit 2 rows with B. Knit 4 rows with A. Knit 2 rows with B. * Knit 2 rows A, knit 2 rows B; repeat from * 9 times more. Knit 2 rows A. Knit 4 rows B. Knit 2 rows A. Knit 8 rows B. Knit 2 rows A. Knit 12 rows B. Knit 2 rows A. Knit 16 rows B. Knit 2 rows A. Knit 20 rows B. With B, bind off loosely and as if to knit. To weave in loose end, thread tail into yarn needle and weave through stitches along wrong side of fabric.

BAG

SKILL LEVEL: Beginner

SIZE: 15 × 11½"

MATERIALS:
Elmore-Pisgah, Peaches & Crème, 100% cotton, double-worsted-weight yarn (400 yards per cone): 1 cone each of Verde Green (53) for color A and Apple Green (51) for color B
Size 10 (6 mm) knitting needles or size needed to obtain gauge
Two stitch markers
Yarn needle

GAUGE:
In St st (knit RS rows, purl WS rows), 14 stitches and 20 rows = 4"/10 cm.
TAKE TIME TO CHECK YOUR GAUGE.

INSTRUCTIONS:
Note: When changing yarn color after 2 rows, carry yarn up side of work.
With color A, cast on 52 stitches. Knit 8 rows for Garter stitch band, noting first row is right side.

Work in St st, beginning with a purl row and changing colors at beg of rows as follows:
5 rows A, 2 rows B
8 rows A, 2 rows B
6 rows A, 2 rows B
4 rows A, 2 rows B
* 2 rows A, 2 rows B; repeat from * 6 times more, 2 rows A
4 rows B, 2 rows A
6 rows B, 2 rows A
8 rows B, 2 rows A, 5 rows B
Knit 8 rows with B for Garter stitch band.
Handles
Bind off 10 stitches, with 1 stitch on right needle, knit 4 more stitches, bind off 22 stitches, with 1 stitch on right needle knit 4 more stitches, bind off 10 stitches.
For first side of handle: With WS facing, join B in first stitch, knit 5. Knit 50 rows. Bind off. Work second side of handle as for first. Sew ends together.
Second Handle: With RS facing, skip first 10 stitches, with A pick up and knit 5 stitches. Knit 50 more rows. Bind off. **For second side of handle:** With RS facing, skip 22 stitches to left of first half of handle, with A pick up and knit 5 stitches. Knit 50 more rows. Bind off. Sew ends together.

FINISHING
Holding RS together, sew side seams. Weave in loose ends along WS of fabric. Turn RS out.

181

easy crochet hat and bag

photo on page 171

SKILL LEVEL: Easy

SIZE: Bag measures approx 8½" across base and stands approx 10" tall, excluding straps. Hat has a circumference of approx 21½" and measures approx 7" from crown to folded brim.

MATERIALS:
Elmore-Pisgah, Peaches & Crème, 100% cotton, worsted-weight yarn (2.5 ounces per ball): 3 balls of Brick Red (96) for MC and 1 ball of Aztec (177) for color A
Size F/5 (3.75 mm) crochet hook or size needed to obtain gauge

GAUGE:
In sc, 16 sts and 16 rnds = 4"/10 cm.
TAKE TIME TO CHECK YOUR GAUGE.

SPECIAL ABBREVIATIONS:
MB (make bobble): 5 dc in next sc, remove hook and then insert it from front to back and into first dc, take lp through, ch 1 to close.
Sc3tog: Draw up a lp in each of next 3 sts, yo and draw through all 4 lps on hook.

INSTRUCTIONS
BAG
Note: Rnds are not joined unless otherwise directed.

BASE
Beg at the base with MC, ch 2.
Rnd 1: 4 sc in 2nd ch from hook.
Rnd 2: 2 sc in each sc around —8 sts.
Rnd 3: As Rnd 2—16 sts.
Rnd 4: (Sc in sc, 2 sc in next sc) around—24 sts.
Rnd 5: (Sc in next 2 sc, 2 sc in next sc) around— 32 sts.
Rnd 6: (Sc in next 3 sc, 2 sc in next sc) around—40 sts.
Rnd 7: (Sc in next 4 sc, 2 sc in next sc) around—48 sts.
Rnd 8: (Sc in next 5 sc, 2 sc in next sc) around—56 sts.
Rnd 9: (Sc in next 6 sc, 2 sc in next sc) around—64 sts.
Rnd 10: (Sc in next 7 sc, 2 sc in next sc) around—72 sts.
Rnd 11: (Sc in next 8 sc, 2 sc in next sc) around—80 sts.
Rnd 12: (Sc in next 9 sc, 2 sc in next sc) around—88 sts.
Rnd 13: (Sc in next 10 sc, 2 sc in next sc) around—96 sts.
Rnd 14: (Sc in next 11 sc, 2 sc in next sc) around—104 sts.
Rnd 15: (Sc in next 12 sc, 2 sc in next sc) around—112 sts.
Rnd 16: (Sc in next 13 sc, 2 sc in next sc) around—120 sts.
Base should measure approx 8½" across.

TOP
Rnd 1: Working in back lps for this rnd only, (sc in each of next 11 lps, MB in next lp) around—10 bobbles.
Rnd 2: Working in both lps, (sc in each of next 11 sc, sc in ch-1 sp behind bobble) around.
Rnds 3–7: Sc in each sc around.
Rnd 8: (Sc in each of next 11 sc, MB in next sc) around; join with sl st in first sc then with A, ch 3 (counts as dc). Fasten off MC.
Rnd 9: With A, dc in each sc around. At end of rnd, join with sl st in 3rd ch of beg ch-3, with MC, ch 1. Fasten off A.
Rnd 10: With MC, sc in each of first 5 dc; (MB, sc in each of next 11dc) around, ending MB, sc in last 6 sc.
Rnd 11: Sc in first 4 sc; (sc3tog, sc in next 9 sc) around, ending sc3tog, sc in last 5 sc—100 sts.

Rnd 12: Sc in each sc around.
Rnd 13: (Sc in next 9 sc, MB) around. At end of rnd, change to A. Fasten off MC.
Rnd 14: As Rnd 9.
Rnd 15: With MC, sc in each of first 4 dc; (MB, sc in next 9 dc) around, ending MB, sc in last 5 dc.
Rnd 16: Sc in first 3 sc; (sc3tog, sc in each of next 7 sc) around, ending sc3tog, sc in last 4 sc—80 sts.
Rnd 17: Sc in each sc around.
Rnd 18: (Sc in next 7 sc, MB) around. At end of rnd, change to A. Fasten off MC.
Rnd 19: As Rnd 9.
Rnd 20: Sc in first 3 dc; (MB, sc in next 7 dc) around, ending MB, sc in last 4 dc.
Rnd 21: Sc in first 2 sc; (sc3tog, sc in next 5 sc) around, ending sc3tog, sc in last 3 sc—60 sts.
Rnd 22: Sc in each sc around.
Rnd 23: (Sc in next 5 sc, MB) around. At end of rnd, change to A. Fasten off MC.
Rnd 24: As Rnd 9.
Rnd 25: Sc in next 2 dc; (MB, sc in next 5 dc) around, ending MB, sc in last 3 dc.
Rnds 26–30: Sc in each st around.
Rnd 31: Ch 3, (counts as dc); dc in each sc around. At end of rnd, join with sl st in top of ch 3.

FIRST STRAP

Row 1 (RS): Ch 1, sc in same st as joining, sc in each of next 14 dc—15 sts; turn.
Row 2: Ch 1, sc in each sc across; turn.
Rows 3–4: As Row 2.
Row 5: Ch 1, sk first sc, sc in each sc across to last 2 sts, sk next sc, sc in last sc; turn.
Rows 6–8: Ch 1, sc in 13 sc; turn.

Row 9: As Row 5.
Rows 10–12: Ch 1, sc in 11 sc; turn.
Row 13: As Row 5.
Rows 14–16: Ch 1, sc in 9 sc; turn.
Row 17: As Row 5.
Rows 18–20: Ch 1, sc in 7 sc; turn.
Row 21: As Row 5.
Rows 22–24: Ch 1, sc in 5 sc; turn.
Row 25: As Row 5.
Rows 26–45: Ch 1, sc in 3 sc; turn.
Fasten off after Row 45.

SECOND STRAP

With RS facing, sk 15 dc from First Strap. Join MC with sl st in next dc, ch 1, sc in same dc as joining and in each of next 14 dc; turn. Complete as for First Strap.

TIES (make two)

With A, ch 125 and fasten off. Weave ties over and under groups of 3 dc from Rnd 31, beg and end at center front of bag. Make overhand knots around each set. Tie straps into a square knot.

HAT

Beg at crown, with MC, ch 2.
Rnd 1: In 2nd ch from hook (dc, ch 1) 7 times; join with sl st in first dc.
Rnd 2: Ch 4 (counts as dc + ch-1); (dc, ch 1 in next ch-1 sp, dc, ch 1 in next dc) around, ending dc, ch-1 in ch-1 sp; join with sl st in 3rd ch of beg ch-4—14 dc.
Rnd 3: As Rnd 2—28 sts.
Rnd 4: As Rnd 2—56 sts.
Rnd 5: Ch 4 (counts as dc + ch-1); (dc, ch 1) in each dc around—56 sts; join with sl st in 3rd ch of beg ch-4.
Rnds 6–10: As Rnd 5.

Rnd 11: Ch 1, sc in same dc as joining. Ch 1, sc each ch-1 sp and dc around—112 sts; join with sl st in first sc.
Rnd 12: Ch 1, sc in same sc as joining. (Sc2tog, sc in next sc) around—75 sts; join.
Rnds 13–21: Ch 1, sc in each sc around; join.
Rnd 22: Turn; (ch 1, sl st) in each sc around for rickrack trim. At end, join with sl st and fasten off.

FLOWERS (make three)

Leaving a 6" tail at beg and end, with color A, ch 4; join with sl st to form ring. In ring (ch 5, sl st) 5 times. Fasten off.

FINISHING

Fold brim in half. Position flowers onto brim and over the joining seam. Take flower tails through both layers of fabric and tie into an overhand knot on WS. Trim ends.

summer top

photo on page 172

SKILL LEVEL: Beginner

SIZES: EXTRA-SMALL (S, M, L, XL)
Note: The pattern is written for the smallest size with changes for larger sizes in parentheses. When only one number is given, it applies to all sizes. For ease in working, before you begin, circle the numbers pertaining to the size you are knitting.

Work St st (knit RS rows, purl WS rows) to approx 8½ (9, 9, 9½, 10)" from beg, ending with a knit row.

Set Up for Armholes

Row 1 (WS): K19 (21, 23, 25, 27) sts, p30 (35, 40, 45, 50) sts, k19 (21, 23, 25, 27) sts.

Row 2: Knit across.

Rep Rows 1-2 for 4 times more, then rep Row 1 again.

Armhole Shaping

Bind off first 11 (13, 15, 17, 19) sts, knit across to last 11 (13, 15, 17, 19) sts and bind off these sts—46 (51, 56, 61, 66) sts rem. Fasten off, leaving a long tail for sewing.

Upper Body

With the WS facing, join yarn, k8, p30 (35, 40, 45, 50), k8.

Row 1: Knit.
Row 2: K8, p across, ending k8.
Rep Rows 1–2 twice more. Knit 12 rows across all sts.

Neck Shaping

With RS facing, k8, bind off center 30 (35, 40, 45, 50) sts, with one stitch on needle, k7 more sts.

Right Strap

Knit every row for Garter St until piece measures approx 17 (17½, 17½, 18, 18½)" from beg, ending with a WS row. Bind off.

Left Strap

With the WS facing, join yarn and k8. Complete as for Right Strap.

FRONT

As for Back.

FINISHING

Sew side and strap seams. Weave in loose ends along WS of fabric.

FINISHED MEASUREMENTS:

Bust: 30 (34, 38, 42, 46)"
Length: 17 (17½, 17½, 18, 18½)"

MATERIALS:

Classic Elite, Provence, 100% mercerized Egyptian cotton, DK-weight yarn (256 yards per hank): 2 (2, 2, 2, 3) hanks of Red (2658)
Size 8 (5 mm) knitting needles or size needed to obtain gauge
Yarn needle
Stitch marker

GAUGE:

In Stockinette Stitch (St st), 18 sts and 22 rows = 4"/10 cm.
TAKE TIME TO CHECK YOUR GAUGE.

INSTRUCTIONS:
BACK

Beginning at the lower edge, cast on 68 (77, 86, 95, 104) sts. Knit 13 rows for Garter St band.
Next Row: Purl across.

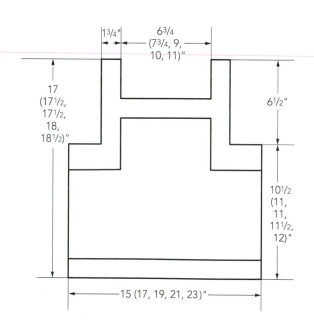

1¾"

6¾" (7¾, 9, 10, 11)"

17 (17½, 17½, 18, 18½)"

6½"

10½ (11, 11, 11½, 12)"

15 (17, 19, 21, 23)"

COMMON ABBREVIATIONS

Note: Less common abbreviations are defined at the beginning of patterns referring to such terms.

KNIT ABBREVIATIONS

approx	approximately
beg	begin(ning)
CC	contrasting color
cn	cable needle
cont	continue
dec	decrease
dpn	double-pointed needle
est	established
inc	increase
k	knit
k2tog	knit 2 together
lp	loop
M1	make one stitch
MC	main color
p	purl
pat	pattern
psso	pass the slipped stitch over
p2sso	pass 2 slipped stitches over
p2tog	purl 2 together
rem	remain(s)(ing)
rep	repeat
rnd(s)	round(s)
RS	right side
tog	together
skp	slip, knit, pass over
sl	slip
ssk	slip, slip, knit
ssp	slip, slip, purl
st(s)	stitch(es)
St st	stockinette stitch
yb	yarn back
yf	yarn forward
yo	yarn over
WS	wrong side

CROCHET ABBREVIATIONS

beg	begin(ning)
ch	chain
dc	double crochet
dec	decrease
est	established
hdc	half double crochet
inc	increase
lp(s)	loop(s)
rep	repeat
rev sc	reverse single crochet
rnd	round
RS	right side
sc	single crochet
sl st	slip stitch
sp(s)	space(s)
st(s)	stitch(es)
tog	together
tr	treble crochet
WS	wrong side

knitting basics

Pattern Sizes

Sizes for each of the projects in this book are noted at the beginning of the instructions. When one size is written out in capitalized letters, it is to note the size of the modeled garment. The instructions are written for the smallest size with changes for larger sizes in parentheses. When only one number is given, it applies to all sizes. For ease in working, before you begin, circle the numbers pertaining to the size you are knitting or crocheting.

Metric Conversions

To convert inch measurements to centimeters, multiply the inches by 2.5.

Needles and Gauge Notations

The needle you choose affects the gauge, or stitches and rows per inch, of your finished knitting.

Knitting Needles

Knitting requires at least two knitting needles to make the knitted fabric. Knitting needles usually are pointed at one end and have a knob at the other. They're available in plastic, bamboo, wood, steel, and aluminum.

Gauge Notations

Most patterns include a gauge notation. The gauge, or the number of stitches or rows per inch, is determined by the size of the needles and the weight of the yarn. Always work a gauge swatch to see whether your tension equals the gauge specified in the instructions. If you have too many stitches per inch, you are working too tightly: Change to larger needles. If you have too few stitches per inch, you are working too loosely: Change to smaller needles. For practice sessions, choose medium-size needles (size 8 or 9) and a smooth, light-color yarn so you can see your work easily.

basics continued on page 186

Button Selection Tips

- To create the proper buttonhole size, buy the buttons before you start the buttonholes.
- Take your gauge swatch when buying buttons; it's a better visual than a skein of yarn.
- If you can't find a good color match, choose a contrasting color.
- Glassy, glittery buttons work well with dressy yarns. Bone, wood, or metal is good for heavy, outdoor garments.
- Buttons are made with or without a shank. Shank buttons are suitable for all yarn weights and are the best choice for thick, bulky knits.
- Buy washable buttons if you plan to wash the garment, and dry-cleanable ones if the garment requires dry-cleaning. Pay attention to special-care instructions that come with the buttons.

knitting techniques

MAKING A SLIPKNOT

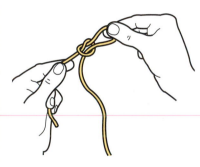

This basic knot comes in handy for other than knitting and crochet too.
Step 1 Let the tail of the yarn hang in front of your palm, and loop the yarn loosely around the first two fingers of your left hand.
Step 2 Pull the yarn attached to the ball underneath the yarn behind your fingers and then through the loop.

Step 3 Hold the tail of the yarn in your left hand and the newly made loop in your right hand. Pull the tail to tighten, and make a slipknot.

CABLE CAST-ON

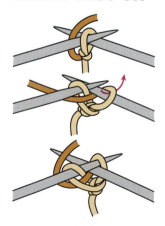

Step 1 Make a slipknot on the left needle.

Step 2 Working into the loop of the knot, knit a stitch; transfer it to the left needle.
Step 3 Insert right needle between the last two stitches. Knit a stitch and transfer it to the left needle. Repeat this step for each additional stitch.

KNIT STITCH

Step 1 Insert the right-hand needle from front to back into the first stitch on the left-hand needle. Notice that the right-hand needle is behind the left-hand needle.

Step 2 Form a loop by wrapping the yarn under and around the right-hand needle.

Step 3 Pull the loop through the stitch so the loop is in front of the work.

Step 4 Slip the first or "old" knit stitch over and off the tip of the left-hand needle.

M1 (make one stitch)
An increase worked by lifting the horizontal thread lying between the needles and placing it onto the left needle. Work the new stitch through the back loop.

PURL STITCH

Step 1 With yarn in front of the work, put the right-hand needle from back to front into the first stitch on the left-hand needle.

Step 2 Form a loop by wrapping the yarn on top of and around the right-hand needle.

Step 3 Pull the loop through the stitch to make a new purl stitch.

Step 4 Slip the first or "old" purl stitch over and off the tip of the left-hand needle.

P1b
Purl through the back loop.

P2togb
Slip two stitches knitwise, one at a time, from the left needle to the right needle. Return these two slipped stitches to the left needle. Purl the two stitches together through the back loops.

GRAFTING STOCKINETTE STITCHES TOGETHER

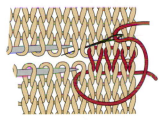

Hold wrong sides together with the needles pointed to the right, thread yarn tail into yarn needle. * Insert needle knitwise through the first stitch on front needle and let the stitch drop from the needle. Insert needle into the second stitch on front needle purlwise and pull yarn through, leaving the stitch on the needle. Insert needle into the first stitch on the back needle purlwise and let it drop from the needle. Insert needle knitwise through second stitch on the back needle and pull the yarn through, leaving the stitch on the needle. Repeat from * across until all stitches have been joined. Adjust tension as necessary. Weave in loose ends.

3-NEEDLE BIND-OFF

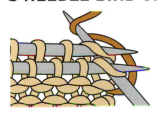

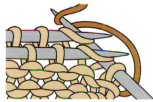

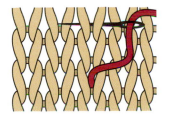

With RS tog, hold in one hand two needles with an equal number of stitches on each and with points in same direction. Using a third needle of the same size, knit together one stitch from each needle. * Knit together next stitch from each needle, pass first stitch worked over second to bind off; repeat from * across to bind off all stitches.

DUPLICATE STITCH

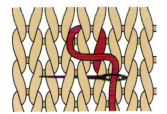

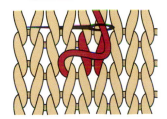

This embroidery stitch imitates the knit stitch, covering the original stitch with a secondary color of yarn to create the pattern. When small areas of color are desired, this is an easy way to add it.

GLOSSARY FOR DECREASING

Knit two together (k2tog): A single decrease, with the facing stitch (the one on top) slanting right. Working from front to back, insert the right-hand needle into the second, then the first stitch on the left-hand needle. Knit both stitches together.

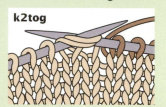
k2tog

Purl two together (p2tog): A single decrease, slanting to the right when viewed from the knit side. With the purl side of the work facing you, insert the right-hand needle, purlwise, through the first two stitches on the left-hand needle. Purl both stitches together.

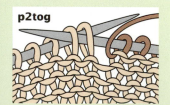
p2tog

Slip, slip, knit (ssk): A single decrease, with the facing stitch slanting left. Slip the first two stitches knitwise, one at a time, from the left-hand needle to the right-hand needle. Insert the left needle tip into the fronts of both stitches, from left to right, and knit them together.

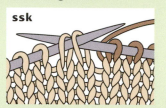
ssk

Slip, slip, purl (ssp): A single decrease, slanting to the left when viewed from the knit side. With the purl side of the work facing you, slip two stitches knitwise, one at a time, from the left-hand needle to the right-hand needle. Return the slipped stitches to the left-hand needle, purlwise. Purl both stitches together through the back loops.

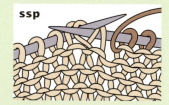
ssp

DECREASE TIPS

Although decreases are usually made on right-side rows, they sometimes occur on wrong-side rows. The following are some general examples.

- **Right-Slanting Decrease:** On right-side rows, knit two together (k2tog). Use purl two together (p2tog) on wrong-side rows.
- **Left-Slanting Decrease:** The slip, slip, knit (ssk) is used on right-side rows. Use slip, slip, purl (ssp) on wrong-side rows. Work decreases at least one stitch in from the edges to maintain even edges for seaming or picking up stitches.

crochet techniques

SINGLE CROCHET

Step 1 Insert the hook into the second chain so that two strands are over the top of the hook and one strand is under the hook.

Step 2 Wrap the yarn over the hook; then pull a loop through the chain. (There should be two loops on the hook.)

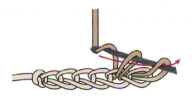

Step 3 Wrap the yarn over the hook and pull a loop through the two loops.

REVERSE SINGLE CROCHET

(Also known as Crab Stitch) Working from left to right, rather than from right to left, ch 1, single crochet in each single crochet around.

HALF DOUBLE CROCHET

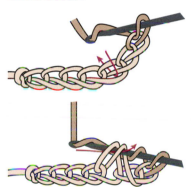

Step 1 Wrap the yarn over the hook; then insert the hook into the third chain from the hook.

Step 2 Wrap the yarn over the hook; then pull a loop through the chain. (There should now be three loops on the hook.)

Step 3 Wrap the yarn over the hook; then draw a new loop through all three loops on the hook.

DOUBLE CROCHET

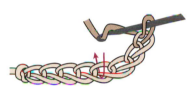

Step 1 Wrap the yarn over the hook; then insert the hook into the fourth chain from the hook.

Step 2 Wrap the yarn over the hook; then pull a loop through the chain. (There should now be three loops on the hook.)

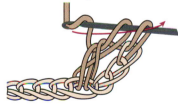

Step 3 Wrap the yarn over the hook; then pull a loop through the first two loops. (There should now be two loops on the hook.)

Step 4 Wrap the yarn over the hook; then pull a loop through the remaining two loops on the hook.

TREBLE CROCHET

Step 1 Wrap the yarn over the hook two times; then insert the hook into the next chain.

Step 2 Wrap the yarn over the hook and pull a loop through the chain. (There should now be four loops on the hook.)

Step 3 Wrap the yarn over the hook and pull a loop through two loops, leaving three loops on the hook.

Step 4 Wrap the yarn over the hook and pull through two loops, leaving two loops on the hook.

Step 5 Wrap the yarn over the hook and pull through the two remaining loops.

189

basic knitting tools

Use the tools shown for knitting projects. Pack a basic tool kit (including the needles for the project) that you can move easily from one project bag to the next.

A Flexible straight needles

B Tape measure

C Knitting needle point protectors

D Circular needles

E Tapestry needles

F Double-pointed needles (dpns)

G Thread-cutter pendant

H Row counters (two styles)

I Stitch marker rings

J Split-ring markers

K Cable needle

L Crochet hook (for picking up dropped stitches)

M Stitch holder

N Knitting gauge

O Spool knitter and needle (for trims)

index

sources

Aurora Yarns
2385 Carlos St.
P.O. Box 3068
Moss Beach, CA 94038-3068
(800)637-3207

Berroco, Inc.
P.O. Box 367
Uxbridge, MA 01569
(800)343-4948

Brown Sheep Co., Inc.
100662 CR 16
Mitchell, NE 69357
(800)826-9136

Classic Elite Yarns
300 Jackson St.
Lowell, MA 01852
(800)343-0308

Coats & Clark
8 Shelter Dr.
Greer, SC 29650
(800)648-1479

Elmore-Pisgah, Inc.
204 Oak St.
Spindale, NC 28160
(800)633-7829

Lion Brand Yarn Co.
34 W 15th St.
New York, NY 10011
(800)871-9810

Muench Yarns & Buttons
285 Bel Marin Keys Blvd #J
Novato, CA 94949-5724
(800)733-9276

Patons
320 Livingstone Ave. S
Listowel, ON N4W 3H3
Canada
(519)291-3780

designer credits

To read more about our team of talented designers, see page 7.

Designers

Svetlana Avrakh—Pages 21, 34–35, and 164–167.

Gayle Bunn—Pages 118–121, 156–158, 160–163, 169, and 174–175.

Lily Chin—Pages 108–109.

Zandy Engelhart—Page 11.

Lidia Karabinech—Pages 30–31.

Valerie Love—Pages 28–29, 32–33, 170, and 172.

Charlotte Quiggle—Pages 22–23.

Ellen Sheckler—Page 11.

Ann E. Smith—Pages 12–20, 24–27, 36–37, 110–117, 122–127, 159, 168, 171, and 174–175.

Kathy Zimmerman—Pages 106–107.